AN ADVANCED STUDENTS' GUIDE TO EDWARD BAUGH'S POETRY

Edward Baugh

Shirlene J. Woodburn, M.A.

An Advanced Students' Guide to

Edward Baugh

Edward Baugh's Poetry

Shirlene J. Woodburn, M.A.

First Edition

10 9 8 7 6 5 4 3 2 1

All LMH titles, imprints and distributed lines are available at special quantity discounts for bulk purchases for sales promotion, premiums, fund-raising, educational or institutional use.

Edited by: K. Sean Harris
Cover Design & Layout: Keneisha Arch

Published by: LMH Publishing Limited
Suite 10-11
Sagicor Industrial Park
7 Norman Road
Kingston C.S.O., Jamaica
Tel.: (876) 938-0005; Fax: (876) 759-8752
Email: lmhbookpublishing@cwjamaica.com
Websites: www.lmhpublishing.com & www.lmhdigital.com

Printed in the U.S.A. ISBN: 978-976-8245-29-8

NATIONAL LIBRARY OF JAMAICA
CATALOGUING-IN-PUBLICATION DATA

Woodburn, Shirlene J.
An advanced students' guide to Edward Baugh's poetry / Shirlene J. Woodburn

p. ; cm.

ISBN 978-976-8245-28-1 (ebk)
ISBN 978-976-8245-29-8 (pbk)

1. Baugh, Edward – Criticism and interpretation 2. Jamaican poetry
I. Title

811 dc 23

Dedicated

to Edward Baugh

"For the zeal of thine house hath eaten me up . . ."

CONTENTS

PREFACE

This text is the result of the author's zeal to foray a path for the extensive study of Edward Baugh's poetry, especially for the advanced student. This project also seeks to foreground in the intellects of an emerging generation of students, the indispensable work of Baugh, in the development of Caribbean literary perspectives, and in so doing expose them to Baugh's poetry as an appreciable branch of his literary contribution. This guide will also be marginally useful to exceptional students at a lower academic level. Due to its ample thematic foci, it is anticipated that interests, other than purely literary, will be emboldened in the quest to reap from the legacy of Baugh's work, overall.

It must be clearly noted, that this *Advanced Students' Guide to Edward Baugh's Poetry* does not attempt to provide a critical analysis of each poem in the newer, *Black Sand,* nor in the prior collection, *It Was the Singing.* Neither does it seek to present any exclusive analysis on any poem. Readers are encouraged to develop greater critical thoughts and 'new' ideas—to delve deeper into what Baugh's poetry is able to offer—and many do offer critical ideas on sustainable living and development. One significant factor to keep in mind is that Baugh is not a poet who is 'chained' to poetic conventions—such as rhythm, rhyme and metre. This guide suggests that a study using such an approach may well thwart, than encourage, the experience.

It has been observed that many of our students are afraid of poetic analyses, and that prose and drama are more affably contemplated. Yet, poetry being a reservoir for culture (contemporary and historical), is a legitimate vehicle for the journey toward personal and collective consciousness, and holds a wealth of information which supports historical research. It is also a vital resource for communicative development, especially for honing critical reading, thinking and writing in students. It is with these things in mind that this advanced students' [study] guide has been prepared.

PART ONE

EDWARD BAUGH

On May 29, 2001, Edward Baugh was honoured in a public function at the University of the West Indies, Mona, Jamaica, for thirty-six years of service in Literatures in English.[1] The occasion marked Baugh's official retirement. Subsequently, a brief biography on Baugh was published in the *Outlook Sunday Magazine* in July (2001).[2] Yvonne Grinam-Nicholson, contributing writer, entitled the special feature: "Professor Edward Baugh: Living the Years". In the article, Baugh is described as someone with an "absolutely critical leadership force" (9) which is especially observed by the manner in which he brought the English department through a transition observed by Professor Mervyn Morris to have been "a decolonization of the department" (9). Where teaching is concerned, Michael Bucknor's comment is that Baugh is a person with the prowess to have "transformed ordinary minds" (9). Baugh's accomplishment as a renowned poet was especially celebrated at the occasion, along with his venerated position as University Orator.

A synopsis of Baugh's private life was also published. Baugh was born in January 1936 in Portland, Jamaica, "in a house near the wharf" (Grinam-Nicholson 9). It is important to make note that several of Baugh's poems reflect on the circumstances and setting of a life in a town near the sea. The evolution of Baugh's intellectual career started with his first scholarship in 1954 to attend the University College of the

1. I was present as a member of the audience for the entire function.
2. In the Jamaica *Gleaner*.

West Indies (UCWI) for the honours degree in English.[3] Since that significant event Baugh has flourished as a Caribbean intellectual with international recognition.

As a writer, Baugh is said to possess a "compendious knowledge of West Indian literature and criticism [with] personal experience of the cultural wars of the 1960s and the 1970s" (JWIL 2)[4]. Baugh, himself, says: "Writing, all art, is a construction of identity through performance".[5] It is, therefore, on the premise of the author's own words, that the investigation of his personal work is launched, to see whether there are any aspects of his known personal characteristics reflected in his poetry, as well as, Caribbean, and Jamaican prototypes.

In his Plenary Address at the second Caribbean Culture Conference UWI, Cave Hill, Baugh spoke about "(Re)Thinking Caribbean Culture".[6] In his conclusion, Baugh elaborated on his personal "desire" (10). He wants to see Caribbean peoples cross their cognitive limitation of otherness—move past, or perhaps out of "decolonization" and firmly establish their identity (10). Still, our own internal tensions challenge us so that there are "many Caribbeans" (11). The problem lies "within the mode of language" (11) and, therefore, there must be changes in "scholarship and pedagogy [so that the] 'literary' and the 'popular' [come] into active relationship" (11). It is a theory for a "model" which would "influence" the world (11). We would not, then, see exclusions in our literature for all would be represented in scholarship and pedagogy.

Is Baugh arguing, then, for a seamless Caribbean—a Caribbean without "marginalization and rejection" (12) in culture, as well as, in the academy? This could be a formidable challenge for academia, for it means that ideas concerning 'good' and 'bad' Caribbean literature would have to be shelved. Baugh states that the primary theorists previously mentioned[7] have not provided any cure for the "specific socio-economic ills of the Caribbean [even though] they are fraught and plangent with a deep awareness of those ills and their historical roots, and of a capacity for healing that is as real as those ills" (12). However, the question that I ask is: "is this restoration of our shattered

3. A comprehensive profile of Edward Baugh has been published in the November 2006 edition of the *Journal of West Indian Literature* and his biography is available on the internet, as well as, in the *Outlook Sunday Magazine* (July 2001). I, therefore, deem it unnecessary to reproduce the details here.
4. Editorial profile on Baugh in the *Journal of West Indian Literature* (JWIL).
5. (Edward Baugh, 23rd Annual Conference on West Indian Literature, 2004)
6. June 4-8, 2001
7. Namely, Walcott, Glissant, Benítez-Rojo, Brathwaite, Harris.

histories possible" (12)?

A few years later[8], Baugh had some rather insightful confessions to make. This was a conference particularly in his honour. It is at this conference that Baugh equated the writer's art with his identity. Baugh looks back, retrospectively, over the twenty-three years since the conference was inaugurated. The theme, then, was "Critical Approaches to West Indian Literature". The Mona Department had thought that it was time (after just a decade of teaching West Indian Literature) Baugh explains, to stop and "take stock of what [they] had been doing, or what [they] thought [they] had been doing" (16).

Another reason for the retrospection was that the respective departments wanted to be on par with contemporary approaches to the teaching of Literature—mainly theoretical approaches[9]. As well, the possibility of building a rapport among university teachers was an objective (of the theme) by which such teachers would hone their skills from their interaction with each other. Since the focus was then on criticism with no obvious thought on pedagogy, Baugh's first confession, is that it was a [serious] mistake—they had in fact failed in their responsibility or duty as educators. Why was it so urgent, or necessary, to elevate themselves as theorists, or even to substantiate the use of theory? In reflecting on this comment of Baugh's, it is worthwhile to consider Frantz Fanon[10] who says that the attitude of the colonized is one of envy of the colonizer (30). Might it not be that literary academics were now a little anxious to move themselves from margin to centre in considering what they thought they had achieved? Is it not feasible that they sought to establish a paradigm for teaching similar to what the colonial 'masters' had brought to the Caribbean? Might it not also be an attempt to empower themselves—thus raising their individual status quo? While the move may have been seen as premature, the intent is not necessarily wrong.

Certainly, the initiative towards "this self-scrutiny" (16) is correlated with the need for empowerment, as Baugh suggests when he says that the participants and the planners of the conference wanted "to make [themselves] more 'state-of-the-art' " (16). Alas, he did not think that West Indian Literary Criticism had, as yet "reached a high level" (16)

8. (23rd Annual Conference on West Indian Literature, Grenada, March 8-11, 2004)
9. The MA by coursework was introduced two years later at Mona, and Literary Theory became the only compulsory course.
10. In *The Wretched of the Earth*

where it could engage in self-criticism since they could not see what was lacking in themselves (meaning the critical approaches). Neither had Baugh seen anything new in any of the critical approaches up to then. So, what benefit, if any, could arise out of that conference?

In looking back at his foreword to the after-conference publication, Baugh reaffirms the "challenge of Theory" (16) which he had indicated, in that it must [11] be seen as only "partial" (17). But, "a head full of theory" guarantees no such acknowledgement. Such acknowledgement can only happen when a person recognizes that "no word is ever final" (17). This suggests, then, that the participants in the conference had not yet clearly understood the nature of theory or how to merge it with the new body of literature then described as West Indian. What Baugh, in retrospect, regrets, is that he had not "call[ed] attention to those landmark statements about ways of seeing West Indian literature which had already appeared" (17). What is certainly implied, is that his observation at that time was shortsighted. It could be that Baugh was also 'guilty' of the same 'blindness' of not yet having reached "a high level" of theoretical "self-awareness" (16) and is now able to look back, on this occasion in his honour, and reflect on his own growth as a literary critic. It can be concluded that by the mid 1960s 'new' ideas concerning West Indian Literature had begun to emerge, and these ideas influenced the body of works we now recognize as Caribbean literature. But, by the early 1980s the evolution in critical thinking had established itself sufficiently for it to be formally recognized at the conference. Caribbean literary writers, then, were well on their way in establishing an identity which was evolving in their literary works. This does not mean, however, that such an identity is an absolutely positive one as it can be seen so far that the metaphors and paradigms created are ambiguous as well as diverse[12].

Baugh may never have thought, back then, that he would have done this recollection—taking his audience back to the 'teething pains' in the development of literary criticism in the chief institutions in the Caribbean. What is clear is how phenomenal the proceedings of that conference were, so that it could be so acutely remembered, and to some extent, re-enacted. Frantz Fanon asserts that "decolonization, which sets out to change the order of the world, is, obviously, a

11. Namely by Wilson Harris (*Tradition and the West Indian Novel,*1964; *The Writer and Society,*1967).
12. Already mentioned in this chapter. Baugh also observes that the revolutionary era of the 1970s+ in the Caribbean influenced this 'new' approach in literary works.

programme of complete disorder" (27). The "order of the [Caribbean] world" was challenged by the changes—one such being Brathwaite's own "rallying-call"—and this largely contributed to 'disorder' at the conference where views 'old' and 'new' clashed. They clashed out of necessity—the "decolonization" was a necessity, as the need to negotiate an authentic sense of selfhood was exigent.

At this point in his recollection, Baugh reflects on the "complexity" of changes, in that even when they are definite one still has to grapple with the realities. He was grappling with a particular reality, the need for a new kind of literature. Baugh suggests that Lashley[13] would have done better in quoting "other bits of [his] review which would have sounded more agreeable to the new dispensation" (20). It would seem, however, that the political agenda of some critics is to promote their own 'theory' by demoting other's. Baugh notes that it was just "a year earlier" that he "argue[d] the Englishness of English literature . . . and the nationalist motive behind the teaching of English literature in England [and so] urge[d] the imperative for West Indians of serious study of West Indian literature" (20). He has led by example.

While the 1971 conference sparked fiery debate, the 1981 conference "did not provoke much direct or sustained engagement with questions of critical theory, or with examination of critical practice" (22). Today, "there is a lot of theoretical sophistication around, thanks especially to the younger generation" (22). But Baugh makes a somewhat cryptic remark when he says:

> Never mind that the academy has not produced its own brand-name theory . . . [and], never mind, either, the programmatic applications of theory which seemed driven only by the will to show that this or that theory had been mastered, and how this or that text may be made to fit it all too neatly, without any conviction as to the necessity of the application. (22)

Might there be a warning in this, concerning how we (mis)use theory? May this be a pitfall in the 'innovation' of the "younger generation"? Baugh then gives commendation to "instances where transatlantic theories are used originally, and interrogated in the process of being appropriated to the Caribbean situation"[14] (22).

13. A participant in an antagonist mode.
14. He makes special reference of Evelyn O'Callaghan's *Women's Writing in the West Indies* (2003). I also make note of how Anderson's *Imagined Communities* is used in this guide.

While Baugh presents his own critical views on Theory, he acknowledges that it has not been easy "deal[ing] with the challenge, or threat, or liberation of Theory" (22). He notes that "most of the truly original and seminal West Indian statements of theory have come from writers who are outside the academic discipline of literary criticism" (22). One such writer, "Walcott, is expressly snide about critics and contemptuous of Theory"[15] (22). This text validates Baugh's depictions of the collective colonial history and does not (in this context) support Derek Walcott's ideas in "The Muse of History" (1978) that such a writer (as Baugh) is chained to the past as a "victim". Nonetheless, Baugh concedes that "we are all theorists" and this does not deny or hinder criticism. He recognizes Rohlehr and Morris as two of the greatest critical contributors in Caribbean literature.

Baugh explains how West Indian and Caribbean criticism can be understood in different contexts: West Indian refers to "Anglophone Caribbean" while "Caribbean" includes both groups. However, Baugh notes that "Caribbean reflects a significant partial shift in how we read West Indian Literature" (24).

Finally, Baugh makes some comments on the theme[16] of this conference. He notes that there are "many different kinds of tradition [and] critical traditions are generated or influenced by all sorts of agencies"[17] (26). Baugh's humorist style surfaces at the close of his address as he speaks of the "difficulty" with its ending—typical of the writing of "novelists and playwrights" (26). Since these belong to the genre of "fiction", he suggests: "perhaps this paper has been a fiction" (26). Still, Baugh asks: "what exactly is Caribbean criticism? (26)" It is the "criticism of Caribbean/West Indian Literature" but the seams 'burst' to accommodate the writings of Caribbean critics on non-Caribbean works. Having forwarded that, the next question he asks is: "who is the critic?" (26). These, too, have not always been "Caribbean persons" (27). At the first conference in 1971 where international persons were present, they watched and heard a spectacle. Thus, Baugh asks: "Are we to regret that that passion has been lost, or are we to recognize that each moment has its own necessity, and that that war was won, to the extent that any war is ever really won?" (27). It would appear that after the struggles, is now the calm.

15. Traditional ideology, hence, Theory of Literature as was first taught in the MA programme.

16. "Caribbean Critical Traditions"

17. One such is *Savacou 3 / 4* (and he credits Mervyn Morris for this reminder).

The question to ask, now, is: Has Baugh written himself in this conference paper? Can we 'read' his identity by this? We read a paper in which Baugh outlines the struggle with various issues—some concerning writers, others concerning criticism, and types of literature. Baugh has presented a panoptic view of the development of literary theory and literature in the Caribbean—it partly explains, too, his own development as a critic, as well as, poet. In his paper is the demonstration of a willingness to change, which means continuous personal interrogation—deconstruction and reconstruction of the self. Humour and candidness are in the tone of his writing, but these do not mask the sense of authority of one who is able to take his reader or listener on a journey to the 'beginning' and back to the present. Baugh does not write as an exclusivist as he privileges original thinking and by example, encourages diversity in thought processes, as well, as applications.

In conclusion, one poet to whose works Baugh has devoted particular critical interest is Walcott[18]. On the occasion of his honoured visit in 1988, he was interviewed by Baugh[19]. Baugh's foremost question to Walcott requires him to speak about "memories or opinions . . . of [his] time as a student [at Mona]" and whether it "mean[s] anything to [him]" (50). It is not coincidence that Baugh shows this interest in the significance of memory.

This interview happened about a decade after Baugh published his critical work on Walcott's *Another Life* in which Baugh examined the idea of *Memory as Vision*. Baugh identifies

> [the] imagery of pathfinding, struggle and survival . . . epiphany and vision . . . the interaction between, on the one hand, the 'real', the actual, the literal, the remembered, the historical, and, on the other hand, imagination, hallucination, dream, vision, art, symbol and myth; the centrality of the concept of 'home'. (2)

Some of these techniques are also exemplified in many of Baugh's poems—especially where there is evocation of the merging of the factual with the imaginary or mythical[20] and the theme of remembrance is variously portrayed. Not only that, the volume is interspersed with Baugh's autobiography and nuances of things and events remembered.

18. Walcott formally received the Special Gold Musgrave Medal in May 1988. It was awarded in 1986 by the Institute of Jamaica.
19. The interview is published in the *Jamaica Journal*.
20. Examples: "Sometimes in the Middle of the Story . . ." and "A Rain-washed Town by the Sea".

However, the idea of "pathfinding, struggle, and survival" (2) is not particularly depicted in any autobiographic detail in *Black Sand*.[21]

Baugh sees Walcott's life as central to his[22] work—the matrix in his literary craft. But, Baugh explains that rather than evoking and sustaining "nostalgia and regret" through the past, Walcott's poetry is "informing the present and being informed by it" (3). Walcott's relationship with his past, then, is his inspiration for finding another life in the present.

In addition, Baugh makes an insightful comment when he describes the structure of *Another Life* in that "while *Another Life* is autobiography and the literal-historical parts of it are true to the best of [Walcott's] memory, it is more (and less) than just autobiography, and its truth is not simply historical" (4). Might not that statement be also said of those of Baugh's poems which have obvious evocations of his own life? For while "truth[s]" are re-created as art, in their interpretations they evoke other "truths" and thus become visions of life[23].

Baugh also has a grave concern as regards Caribbean development and the kind of separateness that plagues us[24]. Baugh says that although many of our major writers' works are "fraught and plangent with a deep awareness of those ills and their historical roots" (2004) that affect Caribbean persons, they do not provide solutions. This is suggesting that Baugh is arguing for literature for sustainable living and development. This 'new' brand of literature, however, must run parallel with the evolution of our Caribbean writers, as he earlier contemplates,[25] and many of Baugh's poems do subtly interrogate human tendencies and rectitude. While the past is relevant, his critical addresses point toward the need for individual and collective growth and development through the willingness to change and avoid exclusivity. Baugh's desire is for a seamless Caribbean in the context of language and literature, where no literature is exclusive of others. It is, also, that the present should be informed by the past—not ignored. Baugh's earnest encouragement is also that we should learn to embrace our history without trauma or guilt, and re-create 'new' history from 'old' memories—we can see this apt representation in his memorable work.

21. As well as, the earlier volume, *It Was the Singing* (2001).
22. Walcott's
23. For example, "The Carpenter's Complaint".
24. Also discussed at the 2001 Conference.
25. In his Plenary.

PART TWO

POETIC STYLE

Poetic Style

Edward Baugh, Caribbean intellectual, has spent much of his academic life as a literary critic and a significant portion as University Orator. But, it is quite obvious that while he was doing so, he yielded to the stirrings of his creative imagination, establishing himself as a poet. These poems depict aspects of the personal, the nation, the collective historical consciousness of the Caribbean, a romantic sensibility, death, varying degrees of desire and regret, and world views. Many of Baugh's poems evoke autobiography and though the details are embellished, it is possible to do parallel readings of personal and collective histories. It is, therefore, safe to assert that Baugh narrates aspects of his own lived experience, seen in the narrations of Jamaican folk life which correspond with his biographic record[26]—reinforcing the concept of writing the self—hence, he writes autobiography as art. This is not to suggest, however, that the entire volume is so. What is definite, is that a journey-through-time motif has been established when several poems depicting adolescence to adulthood are linked.[27] We are able to link the poems through the recurring imagery in the combination of sea, town, and folklife. We link them also through specific reference to the Jamaican landscape—named places on the Jamaica map. We also make the link through the distinct voice of the narrator and the Romanticized manner of telling—the warmth which often exudes from the tone and

26. I refer to his published interview in *Outlook,* mentioned in chapter one and information available in other media.

27. As examples are: "A Rain-washed Town by the Sea" (131), "Responsibility" (65), "Sunday Afternoon Walks with My Father" (67), "Small Town Story" (118), "Words" (116).

imagery as the remembrance unfolds. The voice of autobiography is distinctly personal, authoritative, and intimate in tone—varying according to subject matter, while other narrative voices 'perform' in diverse contexts. Throughout, we see the literal constructs merging with the fictional (mythical) in creation of poetry as art. A distinctly recognizable strain in Baugh's poetic craftsmanship is memory, which is evoked in dynamic continua, and the majority of poems reflect remembrance in performance.

The most prolific, autobiographic Caribbean poet is none other than Walcott. Although a few poems in *Black Sand* evoke autobiography, this comparison with Walcott is only to identify a common preoccupation—memory. Baugh's *Memory as Vision* supports the view that Baugh has a predisposition for the psychodymamics of memory—evoked in the words of one poem as "liv[ing] . . . in parenthesis"[28]. As such, his imagination readily identifies this strain in Walcott's work. In a 1975 review of *Another Life* Baugh observes that *Another Life* is "a poem whose concerns include the tyranny of memory" (59). Not so, where Baugh's poetry is concerned, for Baugh's autobiographic poetry evokes no tyranny or trauma. Rather, Baugh's work exudes a Romantic sensibility—gentleness, warmth, bonding, humour, drama, dreaming, and desire, which often mask profound insights. These are offered as his personal style.

Poetic autobiography, complex and subjective though it may sometimes be, has a certain value. It is so because it touches our imagination and allows us to live virtually in the experience evoked through its artistic worth. This is, also, individual though it may be, it often represents a collective experience, as well as, appeals to our humanity. For example, in "Small Town Story" (118), many parallels can be invoked and relevant meanings interpreted—a story that many could tell of themselves. Then, there is the artistic value in such poetry—re-created in poetic form, they become "exhibits"[29] to the world.

Baugh also shares the company of Jamaican poets who write the nation in poetry. The names of landscapes or sites have meaning for those who understand their 'codes', but Baugh also evokes the collective ethos: references to people, places and things which require a knowledge of local geography, history, language, and even social studies. As an example, we read of "Norwich halt" and that "the train traced the curve

28. "Hedge Trimming" (88)
29. Benítez-Rojo

/ of the bay" in "Joe Waugh, Engine Driver" (66). "Norwich halt" cites Portland, and the railway lines are so close to the sea in some parts[30] that only a few strides are needed in order to take a swim. However, years later, "weeds choke the ties, and twilight transfigures / the stained glass windows of the station house / that is now a museum". Why is this so? All across Jamaica, the station houses of the Jamaica Railway Corporation and their supporting buildings have been abandoned, and consequently fallen into Walcott's "disjecta membra"—ruins. The cessation of the Jamaica railway service happened during economic hardships around the 1980s. Also, "stained glass windows" indicate that the station was built under European influence, which grounds colonial rule in the country. Therefore, in this short poem, narratives on the nation are submerged and they are not evoked only by the naming of places. We can also see how Baugh crafts the embodiment of nation in characterization. The mannerisms of Jamaican personae are depicted in poems such as "The Carpenter's Complaint" (120) and "Walking to Jerusalem" (39).

In addition, Baugh's poetry also re-creates Jamaican folklife. The particular idiom of the Jamaican folk in their simplest setting is aptly illustrated in "The Carpenter's Complaint". The oscillation between the vernacular and standard English is representatively Jamaican. In "It Was the Singing" (83) we see a Jamaican folk in what Rohlehr refers to as the "urban continuum"—the cadence in the manner in which the narrative is told, and the failed effort to speak 'proper' is demonstrative of the lack of sophistication inherent in the folk persona. However, this seeming lack of sophistication in the two foregoing poems only mask the awareness of high moral conduct which the speakers convey. Traditional folk life can only be termed 'simple' in the context of lack of modernization. But, their closeness to nature is often enviable. This underscores the idea that many 'folk' and those who practise lifestyles related to the traditional folk see this manner of living as authentic—thus preferred. In addition, these folk narratives are crafted in such a language that they will readily appeal to the larger consciousness or wider community of people. It is significant that Baugh's poems are appealing in their simplicity[31]—as if crafted for a folk sensibility[32]. More significant for consideration is the verisimilitude the poems evoke. As they 'read themselves' through the narratives, the stories are able to 'order' the lives of more people and 'simplicity' is really only at surface

30. I have disembarked the train by the seaside on several occasions in the 1970s.
31. Used here in the sense of diction that is relatively easy to understand.
32. This is in no way suggesting a preferred readership.

level. For this reason, then, I suggest the idea of Baugh as a sophisticated and 'strategic' writer[33].

Like so many Jamaicans, Baugh lived his early life in the traditional folk style. In these poems he represents not just his experiences, but a selective Jamaican consciousness. As the traditional folk migrate to and adopt aspects of urban lifestyle, so we can identify a persona who looks back on his home town and re-names it "Small Town". We hear the voice of a young lad in the wee hours of the morning narrating "Responsibility". We get another vision of folk living in "Yard Boy". These are representations of Jamaican lifestyle which articulate a collective ethos.

Baugh's poetry also represents the Caribbean collective history which is variously depicted metaphorically by our major Caribbean literary writers. The section on Facets of Postcolonial Memory discusses some of the postcolonial evocations in Baugh's work. Of the metaphorical representations that Baugh discusses at the 2001 Caribbean Culture Conference, he is most closely aligned with Walcott and Brathwaite due to imagery and connotations evoking the sea, and Baugh's water imagery extends to imagery of river. As examples, there are "Detail from 'Ritual of the River'"[34] and "Running River Water" (108) which add to the greater preoccupation with sea (water). In this example, we can reflect on the intertextuality of Caribbean texts—possibly through the impact of shared collective colonial experience and Baugh's critical work on other writers—but the extension of the imagery to river could very well mean that Baugh has a heightened sensibility for running water[35].

Some of Baugh's poetry evoke thoughts of the Romantic movement of the 1780s due to their appeal to the imagination, beauty of nature, human desires and spirituality. The latter published poems especially thrill with desires—from ordinary wishful thinking to intense yearning[36]— and several depict unapologetic frankness in tone, even when deeply intimate in subject matter. In some poems, too, death weighs on the imagination as an anchor. The imagery and diction employed in Baugh's poetry are often deceptively simple throughout, and this is an indication of Baugh's ingenuity. This phenomenal attribute should instruct us in our approach.

33. This is more obvious when the language of his poetry is compared with the language of his critical writings.
34. This poem is published in *It Was the Singing* (2000).
35. As the highly imaginative poem "Running River Water" (108) suggests.
36. Published in the first section under "New Poems".

PART THREE

THEMES

INTRODUCTION: REMEMBRANCE AS MUSE

As a graduate student in a course about "Writing the Nation in Poetry"[37] I was emboldened in the quest to determine the extent to which Baugh's poetry depicts Jamaica's oral culture, landscape and history. The narratives passed down through generations by word of mouth are a country's oral culture. These narratives are reservoirs with social, political and geographical evocations—factually and mythically constructed. Jamaica's oral cultural tradition evoke mannerisms that accompany speech acts, and a certain ethos which can be described as a Jamaican sensibility in performance. Some literary constructs such as poetry resonate with orality, yielding more than just a basic understanding of print medium. In this sense, some of Baugh's narrative poetry imitate oral style. This is obvious whether or not the poems are written in dialect, as Baugh has a skill of creating a persona who is 'alive'. This initial intrigue motivated a deeper investigation of the volume and the recurring topos of remembrance was observed. Thus, the idea of the inspiration of poetic craft by remembrance, or memory, emerged. In the topos of remembrance, Baugh re-creates Jamaican folk life, landmarks, landscapes, colonial past, folk tradition and contemporary lifestyle—including politics.

37. Postgraduate studies.

The idea of the inspiration of poetic craft by remembrance, or memory, I, therefore, present to you as Baugh's muse—memory as muse. In that it is definitive, means that this creative force evokes the self—thus autobiographic. This idea of muse is drawn from Greek and Roman mythology, in which it is represented as the goddess or force personified as woman, the source of inspiration for a creative artist. In the specific context of this text, muse is understood to be the energy for artistic recreation or representation. The idea of remembrance or memory[38] working as muse means that the artistic representation—the poetry—is depicted in the mode of memory. Two representations of memory outstanding in Baugh's poetry are mythical (factitious) and factual (based on facts). The mythical aspects are the creative representations which replace an understanding or remembrance of actual history[39]. Factual representations of memory are those of places and events whose existence can be traced[40].

Concerning a writer's propensity to create, Gordon Rohlehr's discussion concerning the inspiration of a work is very useful indeed. It is authoritative in its support of the idea in this text that a work of art can suggest its own interpretation. In "The Problem of the Problem of Form" (1992) Rohlehr observes that "the writer's intelligence, temperament and sensibility" can be detected in the subject matter of the work which is shaped by "the writer's imagination" (1). He further states that "[when] the work of art is its own subject" (1) the process of its creation can be detected. It is in this context the depiction of definitive memory is explored—where memory 'performs' as art and the artistic creation or re-construction of the event is a 'new' form.

In further support of the idea of this particular 'reading' of Baugh's poetry, *The Repeating Island* is an authoritative source wherein the idea of a worldview of literature is reinforced, supporting the view that Baugh's work transcends a strictly Jamaican context, thus enlarging the possibilities for interpretation. In it, Antonio Benítez-Rojo cautions us not to think of literature "as private and quiet as prayer", but as being "one of the most exhibitionist expressions in the world" (22-23). It is, therefore, the privilege of every reader to "transform it, [and] make it [his or her] own" while simultaneously, the text "transforms [the reader] makes [the reader] its own" (Benítez-Rojo 23).

38. Both are used interchangeably in the same context.
39. Such as, "Sometimes in the middle of the Story . . ." (128)
40. Such as, "View from the George Headly Stand, Sabina" (80)

Nonetheless, the most significant theory relevant to the concerns of remembrance as muse is that of Benedict Anderson's "Memory and Forgetting". Memory is essential to human existence and function, and apart from its ordinary function in life, it can be given representative or symbolic properties. A poem, as art, being material, can represent something as intangible as memory. Anderson explores the phenomenon of "Memory and Forgetting" as regards places and people, and although the theory is not primarily defined as Caribbean, it is still a very useful concept.

The main idea being postulated by Anderson's particular theory is that there is a tendency in humans to reproduce which extends beyond the propensity for biological reproduction. According to Anderson, this impulse is also manifested in the act of naming places, but it is also relevant to persons[41] and even events. Citing cities 'new' and 'old' that have been strangely renamed through European exploitation, Anderson concludes that rather than 'new' cities becoming 'successor' or 'inheritor' of 'old' places, as in ancient tradition, this modern phenomenon of naming has created new versions of old cities, coexisting with them (187). The idea being drawn on here is the representation of an 'old' experience in a 'new' form.

Of course, Anderson's idea is not entirely new. Indeed, the articulation of the concept of shaping or re-creating ideas into form is not exclusive to Anderson, but can be traced back to Plato in his *Republic; Book X* where he speaks concerning mimetism. Firstly, where Plato is concerned, ultimate reality lies in the spiritual. The spiritual realm, then, holds the intangible idea—the original—which is the precursor to the manifestation of the idea in form. In the critical analyses of these ideas, memory is seen as the intangible form and the poetic representation is its manifestation. Even in instances where the experience represented is not factual (as being a lived one) the idea for its creation existed before its (poetic) medium. When we understand the idea for a work as being older to its manifestation, which is newer, Anderson's theory of a new representation of the old is related to Plato's in principle.

So, in considering Baugh's poems, we have, in a sense, the imagination of the writer which is intangible, and the artwork which is tangible. Additionally, the poems, as artefacts, are subject to varying degrees of manipulation during the "exhibition" process described by Benítez-Rojo.

41. A child named as a junior, for example, is not the same as his parent, but it is interesting finding out why it is often done.

This idea is crystallized by Mikhail Bakhtin:

> The work and the world represented in it enter the real world and enrich it, and the real world enters the work and its world as part of the process of its creation . . . in a continual renewing of the work through the creative perception of listeners and readers. (254)

That is, there is no limit to how poems, or any work of artistic value might be 'read' or appropriated. While the artist lives, the experience which is stored in his memory lives 'parallel' to its crystallized form—the work, which is the poem—but the potential of the work as artefact will be magnified when the two experiences are no longer parallel.[42] In this context, I consider the imaginary construct—the memory—as old, and its representation in poetic form as new.

Additionally, with respect to "The Biography of Nations" (204) Anderson also illustrates how memory can be replaced by narration, and identity constructed by narrating events from the past into the present; every nation narrates its own past. The role of the artist in his cultural setting is to provide an understanding of past and present culture and his representative mode is not necessarily premeditated. Sometimes the representation is harsh, and at other times mitigated. The understanding of this cultural need—of narrating the past—provides a necessary counter-reading for Walcott's "Muse of History" to provide a balance.

When Walcott speaks of the "[M]use" of history, I understand him to be addressing the memory of an historic event significant enough to evoke a specific artistic response. Where postcolonial depictions of memory are concerned, Walcott's theory in "The Muse of History" is noteworthy. Concerning the colonial past and the ways in which many Caribbean literary artists choose to remember it in their work, Walcott apparently rejects the common practice he observes as a mode of victimization or remorse. Moreover, Walcott subtly invites debate on the effort of writing back (as in writing against) to the colonial master in his own language—indicating that such an action really implies servitude, not victory—hence a self-defeating exercise. It is self defeating, he implies, if the writer's agenda is clearly anti-colonial. [43] Instead, Walcott

42. As is the experience in our culture where artefacts are not only created to represent events, but, also, where they are remnants they also increase in their significance over time. This is also significant after a writer's death.

43. Edward Brathwaite's *The Arrivants* and Dennis Scott's *An Echo in the Bone* are examples of works that re-create the African experience with the colonizer in the New World and depict colonial victimization.

suggests an alternative which is to be found in the memory, in the lived experience of the artist which becomes art. [44]

As regards Baugh, many poems legitimately engage with an artistic representation of collective memory—both factual and mythical. This validates the necessity for a knowledge and understanding of the collective history of the Caribbean region and this history's lasting impact on its culture. Anderson's theory on narration also validates the need for a new generation to acquire a memory of their past. This not only helps them in finding their own negotiable space, but is critical for the establishment of an identity or knowledge of self.

44. This comment is partly inspired by Patricia Ismond's "Another Life: Autobiography as Alternative History." (*Journal of West Indian Literature*. Vol. 4, no. 1, Jan 1990).

Definitive Memories, or Autobiography as Art

The last poem in this collection— "A Rain-washed Town by the Sea"— ends with the following words:

> These memories define me. I keep them
>
> against that morning when my eyes
>
> no longer turn to greet the sun. (131)

It is a poignant way to end. One would think that the 'message' is obvious—that the persona is referring to a time when he becomes physically and mentally passive. Bennett and Royle (1999) ask, "What is an end?" (251). There appears to be no "end", for, "when it comes to reflecting critically on our reading of a literary text, thinking about the end is a good way of starting" (251). This poem, then, provides an insight into the critical reflections in *Black Sand*—signifying the 'beginning' of self-defining poetic constructs cast in the mode of memory.

Remembrance plays a critical role in human behaviour. Whether negatively or positively, memories shape us—personally and collectively. Since memories shape us, they define us. Remembrance—memory—works as muse due to its propensity to define or re-define human behaviour. Remembrance, seen to influence creative processes, is the overarching theme in this *guide*. In a very specific way, "A Rain-washed Town by the Sea" depicts the 'beginning' of a series of personalized narratives which, write/right the individual, the nation, and readers as audience—in respect to their particular contexts[45].

Memories of "mother", nature, and "school" encapsulate the life of the persona while he grew up in "A Rain-washed Town by the Sea". There only is a mere hint of the title in the context of the poem. Indications are that the persona has the "ambition" to leave town at perhaps the best opportunity—seen in the image of the "jet [which] chalks the arrow of [his] ambition". The other haunting image is "the cobalt sea" which, apart from being a literal landscape, interacts with the imagination, is a reservoir for collective history, a metaphor for freedom and an alternative route towards realizing "ambition". It is because of the impression of the sea on the psyche, for instance, that the speaker is able to say, assuredly: "I shall dream / on the cobalt sea."

45. That is, in writing the nation, or righting (justifying) the self—personal identity.

In this instance is landscape as vision—"I shall dream"—not just that "I" will be dreaming (vision), but also of what "I" shall be dreaming (another vision). These dreams in "A Rain-washed Town by the Sea" are later fulfilled in narratives depicting memories of the past—such as in "Small Town Story" (118) when the speaker says, "I return" having "made good". Perhaps this preoccupation with envisioning is one reason that Baugh is able to interpret *Memory as Vision* as the psychodynamics of Walcott's *Another Life.* The image captured in the title "A Rain-washed..." is illustrative when the persona says: "[b]y mid-day it will rain, / extravagantly, the gutters will gurgle with delight". But, one can get a sense of dissatisfaction from reading the last two lines, so that it is tempting to search for answers elsewhere.

It might be surprising, to see how the last poem of the volume migrates to its beginning—the first poem—to complete a narrative. Could this be a happy coincidence with Bennett and Royle's observation? When you have completed reading "A Rain-washed Town by the Sea", then flip to the first poem in the volume and you can see a continuation or a transition that appears natural. We see at the beginning, an anticipatory end, in "End Poem" (13).[46] The end is at the beginning, and the beginning is at the end. And so, inherent is the idea of a closed volume—that of a consciousness or awareness in the persona of having charted a course is inescapable.

Early memories are crafted in "Responsibility" (65). In this poem is the voice of a young child narrating the early morning events of rural, country-style, living. The persona seems to say: 'This is one of my first memories of responsibility in action'. This memory is self-defining and is verified when the persona says, "I too some distant morning / shall rise responsibly". Although the poem has fourteen lines, it is an early indication of how Baugh shrugs off the coat of the strict metre and rhyme and re-presents the sonnet in individual style.

This young voice also resonates in speaking of "Sunday Afternoon Walks with My Father"[47] (67) in explaining the paternal, as well as, community bonding memories he experienced. The image of the sea is magnified, and because it is inextricably linked with the persona's memories, it is owned as personal history, and it is a part of the persona's discovery of the self—a part of his identity. For example, very early in the persona's young life he was already "dream[ing] / on the cobalt sea"

46. More about this poem on page 56

47. Analysed later in this chapter.

and on this very special outing with his father "he caught the trick of looking" under the surface of the sea. The sea is mystery and beauty and a metaphor for memory—the depth of the sea holds "memor[ies] . . . [and] glimpse[s] of primeval otherness . . . of weekday worlds". In the same way that memory seems to be held in the deep recesses of our minds, so the sea holds mystery in its depth. The persona looks and 'discovers' other lives in the sea; thus, in the process of discovering the self, we also discover others. These experiences are representative—transcending the privileged "I" and embracing world view.

Most, if not all, Jamaicans who grew up during the early to mid twentieth-century should remember that around that time, green bananas were a chief export crop, especially to England[48]. Hence, the image of "a human millipede hurrying the green / bunches into the sure hands of stevedores" is that of the loading of bananas onto the ship for export. In this specific image, Baugh, again writes the nation's—Jamaica's—history in poetry. More than two-thirds of a century later, banana export has fallen significantly due to trade policies on the one hand, and the effects of natural disasters, on the other.

Summarily, it is this same town which is figured in "The Town That Had Known Better Days" (69). We know that the "marlin" is a deep sea fish, but "the *Zacca,* which idled / in the haven of our picturesque, ramshackle port / like some migratory sea-bird / nesting between oceanic flights" is an even more concrete image of a town by the sea. This town gets its 'new' name as "A Rain-Washed Town by the Sea" and Baugh re-creates it in a narrowed visionary[49] context.

The image of impending flight seen in "A Rain-Washed Town by the Sea"[50] is crystallized in "Small Town Story" (118). The sense of distancing with which this narrative begins is indicative that the speaker did not share the "pre-adolescent dreams" of his friends. Any idea that the speaking voice could be anything other than male is dispelled by this final definitive narrative about "Small Town". The very first verse is about "wives they envisioned" in their "mannish chat" and the games they played were "cricket and cowboys". In fact, throughout the poem a binary structure is maintained between false hopes and reality, success and failure.

48. Baugh's biography tells us that he was born and grew up in one of Jamaica's chief banana parishes—Portland—which has at least one shipment port. He also lived close to the wharf.

49. A similar observance Baugh makes concerning Walcott's *Another Life.*

50. At the end of the collection.

The sense of distancing (hence, difference) is first introduced by "they"—which casts the narrator in the mould of spectator. "Small Town" has nuances of limitation, inadequacy, and unfulfillment. A 'large' town would have greater possibilities—this personalized image is also individual, as well as, representative—appealing to the collective consciousness (of many like-minded persons) and of humanity's migratory tendencies.

The binary structure of "they" versus "I" is enlarged in the third verse as the persona says, "I return"—having left. He has been labelled "good", by the townsfolk, and the implied narrative is that "they" who were left behind in the town turned out 'bad'. The irony which becomes evident is that though the persona has now become more equipped with words due to his "education" he cannot find words to "span the graceless silences" which hover between himself and his former playmates.

Perhaps this poem depicts the fullest definition of the persona's journey (and development) to selfhood. "Small Town Story" is a retrospective narrative of the then and now—the 'old' and 'new'. The other definitive poems are 'trapped' in narrative 'time', while "Small Town Story" takes us through time. Yet, one cannot ignore the discriminating tones in which the narrator speaks against those who "lingered in the stagnant town [to face a reality of] rum and puke / [a]nd endless, pointless noons to grieve, / [a]nd a plain, fat woman to deceive". The message could easily be that the 'old' can have no communion with the 'new'[51].

Just as the distancing is evident in "Small Town Story", so is the closeness discernible in "Yard-Boy" (113). Recognizing the narrative voice as the same, we are able to make a particular contrast. The voice that speaks in "Yard Boy" reveals that his "boyworld" was significantly influenced by an 'other' boy—one who was his servant, rather than his intellectual peer. This "Yard-Boy" "wielded [his] boyworld"—demonstrating a near absolute degree of influence in the speaker's life. A significant factor is that this boy servant "couldn't read"—yet was able to teach the persona a lesson in hard work, dedication and responsibility. A binary structure is again illustrated. While "Yard-Boy" is strong, the speaker says he grew up contrastingly weak. We see this in the "charles-atlas shoulders" versus "skinny weakling" imagery. We also understand the strength of this 'other' boy in the image of

51. This echoes the Biblical allegory of old and new wines which must have different wineskins.

the "axe'[s] / . . . blade flashing, splitting / wood for the dover stove". Although "he rested" on "Sundays" he still had to "polish . . . shoes". As such, "Yard-Boy" had no real rest day.

At first appearance the narrative appears as a "tribute"—one that suggests the theme of admiration, and as such evokes odes of the Romantic era. However, in the 'submerged narrative' it is reasonable to question how such close association never resulted in the 'other' boy's literacy. Was it cultural conventions that dictated that this servant boy remained illiterate? The persona affirms this illiteracy of the 'other' when he says: "those comic books / he couldn't read"[52]. Also, why is it necessary to "insist" that this particular memory is evoked as "a tribute"?

Other definitive memories are narrated in the poems, "June Roses" (115) and "Words" (116). "June Roses" depicts the image of an "aunt who died young". The first line suggests an epitaph: "Flo, Floris, flower of Eden". She, the "little mother" of the persona's life, "suddenly . . . died". Her beauty and purity invoked by the persona are metaphorically depicted as "June Roses". Her presence provided a spiritual comfort called 'home'. The corresponding poem, "Words", also speaks about mothering and death. The persona says: "My mother loved words". In this situation, however, we see imminent death rather than sudden disappearance by the diagnosis: "metastases". The irony in the situation is that the shock from the knowledge of "metastases" has 'whipped' words into silence.

The foregoing poems are examples of definitive memories as they most closely represent the narrating of lived experiences which influence the persona's development. They also illustrate the merging of the mythical and literal to evoke the effect of memory on the psyche. It is, therefore, safe to assert that Baugh narrates aspects of his own lived experience, seen in the narrations of Jamaican folklife which correspond with his biographical record—reinforcing the concept of writing the self—hence, he writes autobiography as art. This is not to suggest, however, that the entire volume is so. What is definite, is that a journey-through-time motif has been established when several poems depicting adolescence to adulthood are linked.[53] We are able to link

52. Again, this image of comic reading is plainly depicted in "The Warner-Woman"(109) when the speaker refers to himself as "Connoisseur of comics"— underscoring the singularity of the speaking voice throughout the narratives.

53. As examples are: "A Rain-washed Town by the Sea" (131), "Responsibility" (65), "Sunday Afternoon Walks with My Father" (67), "Small Town Story" (118), "Words" (116).

the poems through the recurring imagery in the combination of sea, town, and folklife. We link them also through specific reference to the Jamaican landscape—named places on the Jamaica map. We also make the link through the distinct voice of the narrator and the Romanticized manner of telling—the warmth which often exudes from the tone and imagery as the remembrance unfolds.

Poetic autobiography, complex and subjective though it may sometimes be, has a certain value. It is so because it touches our imagination and allows us to live virtually in the experience evoked through its artistic worth. In addition, individual though it may be, it often represents a collective experience, as well as, appeals to our humanity. For example, in "Small Town Story", many parallels can be invoked and relevant meanings interpreted—a story that many could tell of themselves. Then there is the artistic value in such poetry—re-created in poetic form, they become, "exhibits"[54] to the world.

Critical Thinking

1. What is the nature of poems termed elegies?

a. Which poems in this section are elegies?

b. Read the poem, "For Simon Cole" (114). Consider how the poem represents word craft. How can you analyse "a vase that needs no flower" as no less a craft than the poem itself?

2. Identify at least three poems other than those in this section that depict the re-creation of memory.

How effective are the imagery in the evocation?

54. Benítez-Rojo

Narratives of Folklife, or Folkways

Folkways, folklife, or folk memory, historically alludes to the life and cultural practice of unsophisticated and sometimes semiliterate persons. Historically, intends to point us far back, and envisions a time when certain cultures, of necessity, lived 'close' to nature. We can then compare (then and now) and see how modernization and industrialization have virtually transformed communities over time. Many persons, despite this evolution, have not only continued their traditional cultural lifestyle with economic sophistication and adaptation— passing these practices on to the next generation—they also take their styles of living to the urban areas. The 'folk', then, can not be 'relegated' to the rural backwaters of any country. In addition, practicians of these cultural practices regard themselves as authentic—a truer representation of how life should be lived, hence they are sophisticated in their simplicity. As well, folklife—folk living—can be seen as a concept, as it is also practiced by intellectuals and advanced members of both rural and urban communities. As Rohlehr asserts: "West Indian society is in fluid motion, and often, oscillation, between the two extreme poles of the folk-urban continuum . . . makes it difficult to define [these] terms" (30).

Some practices, however, have changed with the evolution of communities due to modernization. Rather than erode traditional cultural practices, though, modernization (and technology) has made possible the preservation of culture using different media, such as in film making, festivals, and historical sites. Still, there are large communities of persons living simple, ordinary lives and who still observe traditional culture in food and entertainment[55]. Their mode of living, when studied, can reveal interesting historical data often in contrast with contemporary culture[56].

In Jamaica, the Oral Tradition was largely a way of life in some deep rural districts as late as the mid twentieth-century and many villages had no electricity which prevented the use of technology available in the capitals[57]. Much knowledge and instruction were passed down through these narratives—even though some were myths—and they

55. Many of these communities are in the rural areas of Jamaica, for example, and certainly in different parts of the world.

56. For example, there are ceremonies and rituals related to the dead, also, for the newborn infant still practiced in some rural communities.

57. I lived in one such village up to the early 1970s where there were regular story-telling sessions, (usually at nights) and there was no electricity.

often were strategies to control and guide the behaviour of the young[58]. As well, children were taught things that were important for them to remember—hence the activity of memory creation and perpetuation through narration. As these traditional practices wane, we find that the significance of the creative writer (and producer) increases—for example, many Jamaicans have never seen or heard "The Warner Woman" (109) depicted by Baugh.

There are persons who study and record the lifestyles (cultural practices) of the folk,[59] but these practices are also preserved by creative writers such as Baugh, who re-create 'realities' in a 'new' mode. A poem, for example, may depict the verisimilitude of life practices, but in that it is reflecting, or imitating, it is 'new' to the 'old'. In addition, it may re-interpret and re-contextualize certain realities or events. More significant, though, is what the listener or reader is able[60] to extract from the experience. The re-creation of folk knowledge, or the creative construction of folk memory, may reveal an admiration or appreciation for the simplicity of life that these persons live. Or, as in the Caribbean experience, the representation of folk memory may reveal facets of postcoloniality. For these reasons, artistic re-creations of folk life are diverse and a necessary part of the vocabulary of depicting a collective experience in Afro-Caribbean life.

Baugh's poems reflect love and bonding—a kind of longing, and a sense of the treasured past—depicted in folklife and country style living in Jamaica. In these poems, there is a sense of well-being, concerning the situation or the person with whom the persona is interacting. As an example, the narrator in "Responsibility" (65) reveals a contrast or double consciousness in the situation presented. The first split in consciousness is provided in the repetition of the word "half"—the persona being "half" awake in the "half dark". The other idea of duality (also suggesting balance) is seen in the presence of "my mother" and "my father" sharing the "responsibility" of the "house[hold]" and the demands of family life in the country. The persona suggests that country living often provides "sweet, morning sleep", nonetheless, when you become fully of age, you need to "rise responsibly". The mood of warmth and acceptance is provided in the words "comforting blur", "muted dream", "covers close", "smile", "thrill", and "sweet".

58. The story of the "Blackheart Man" is one such.

59. Ethnographers

60. These aspects are discussed in "Facets of Postcoloniality, or Memories of the Collective Historical Consciousness of the Caribbean".

The poem, being fourteen lines, is a reminder of the sonnet, but has an individuality that also suggests a unique and private experience due to the absence of a strict rhyme scheme or traditional structure. In fact, the narration is given in three sentences which evoke the idea of a private experience among three—father, mother and child. The larger picture is that responsibility is taught in the demonstration of responsible behaviour, and the poem is reflective. "Responsibility" depicts the simplicity of folklife which is a reality in the rural Jamaican districts.

A similar idea of responsible conduct is depicted in "Joe Waugh, Engine Driver" (66). "Joe Waugh", however, is crafted in the image of a legendary folk hero—his life filled the town of "Norwich". In the mind of a young boy "Joe Waugh" is larger than life.

The narrative begins with a sense of the controlled excitement and suspense that one experiences, reminiscent of the country and western movie, when the speaker says: "He rode into town / after nightfall". The idea of movie star is communicated, and the mind is prepared to receive an individual extraordinaire. "Joe Waugh", apparently unawares, casts a "spell" on the "townsfolk" who "would say his name like a boast / . . . over their suppers". The "townsfolk" owned him, rather than he owned them, for though he is widely acknowledged, it is with a "genial grunt" that he responds to their "respect" and admiration.

Though, by his routine he 'orders' their lives, he stands, almost aloof, as a god-like figure—revered and untouchable. Additionally, it is with a "hurry" that he leaves town and is gone again before "first light". The memory of the man is indelible even though his admirers are "dead" and "the station house / . . . is now a museum". The word "museum", when crystallized with the figure of "Joe Waugh", merge human persona with history—"Joe Waugh" is re-constructed in mythical fashion in the preservation of history. "Joe Waugh, Engine Driver" depicts a particular era in Jamaica's history when commuters used railway as a major route to travel across the island.

There is another country town that enjoyed excitement of a different nature—"The Town That Had Known Better Days" (69). This narration opens not with the suspense, but with similar excitement of "Joe Waugh, Engine Driver". The affluent movie star image is depicted in the opening of this poem. People say that rumour spreads fast, but that idea is magnified when the persona says: "Errol Flynn's red *mg* raced / like rumour through our town". The expression also allows us to think that rumour travels faster than we think. It is apparently the dramatic arrival of the vehicle which causes the "scattering" since "[h]is pistol" suffices as a metaphor for explosive disruptive sound, as well as, aggressive driving. The metaphor is sustained in the idea of disturbed peace—folklife here being depicted as one of peace and quiet until the disturbing of the balance. It is not so unwelcome a disturbance as may first appear, for while animals "scatter" in fright, folks are eager to catch a glimpse of the performance.

"The Town That Had Known Better Days" evokes boyhood folk memory similar to "Responsibility" and "Joe Waugh, Engine Driver". The memory of those days is re-lived—remembered—in a mode that corresponds with the contemplation of artefact. How one contemplates an artefact would indeed depend on what is known about it and how one is able to relate to it in one's lived experience. The foregoing narratives are told in the first person but not by the same technique. In "The Town That Had Known Better Days" we get a view of "The Town" as if its interrupted history is evolving on a screen—the persona largely being the keen spectator of events—and we know the speaker is involved by the repetitive "we". There is a double vision in this narrative, for when the excitement was over, "the place slipped quietly back to its proper / identity". The town, then, is in a state of degeneration in the present narrative 'time' and the 'sleepiness' and 'listlessness' of some of its inhabitants are depicted in the "scattering / [of] stray dogs and chickens, [and] old rumheads " who cannot face reality—represented by "sunlight". This "Town" which had not always been in this state of degeneration, had 'new life' infused into it—temporarily—by the arrival of the "*Zacca*". Though the narration begins with a sense of excitement and humour, it ends in disappointment and slight distaste.

The voice of a more involved narrator tells the story of "Responsibility". The mood of intimacy is forthright and it is combined with a sense of owning one's history—the sense of acceptance that one's life is being ordered by the example of one's parents. We can see that the speaker lived in the experience of "The Town . . ." but also that years later he 'eyes' it in an abstract manner. A similar sense of abstractedness, though coupled with admiration, narrates the story of "Joe Waugh . . .". "[T]wilight" depicts the nuances with which his name, as well as, "the station house / that is now a museum" can be interpreted, as the speaker relinquishes authority by saying: "I never knew him. He was / only a name".

Again, a strong sense of travelling through time links several of Baugh's poems. For example, in "The Warner-Woman", is evoked the image of travelling on foot, as was mostly done by deep rural folk dwellers in a certain era of Jamaican socio-economic development. Then, in "Joe Waugh, Engine Driver" is depicted an era of railroad travelling and its impact on "the townsfolk". The image of travelling in "The Town That Had Known Better Days" is advanced, that is, from railroad to sports car. When examined in this way, these poems offer a good example of the idea of emergence or evolution of folklife discussed earlier. Not only that, but when structured in this manner, these poems give another version of the nation (Jamaica) in narration[61] in that they chart an aspect of the country's development. The poems are not only reservoirs with personal and collective histories, but as Anderson states in "The Biography of Nations", narration is essential for knowledge to be passed down to the new generation. The poems are artistic constructs for memory re-creation. But, it is also significant to come to the understanding that the journey started by sea—hence, "Sometimes in the Middle of the Story . . ." can be interpreted as the re-construction of the birth of a nation. The 'old' idea for this 'new' construct, regrettably, has its origin in the idea[62] for the Trans-Atlantic Slave Trade.[63]

Subsequently, as the towns evolve, so do their inhabitants. It has been already established that the narrator gives the idea that he, too, has travelled through time. The voice of the persona—the narrator—remains constant due to the images that are related or linked. It is seen that "Small-Town Story" has a clear relationship with "The Town That Had Known Better Days" due to the images of "ship", womanizing, and inebriation which are common to both poems. This town ("Small-Town") is also clearly near the sea due to the fact that the inhabitants are able to turn from "gazing at the sea" to sexual pleasures with women. Again, the image of a town near the sea is communicated in "Joe Waugh, Engine Driver" as "the train traced the curve / of the

61. This idea coincides (unavoidably) with the title *Nation and Narration* (2007) Ed. By Homi K. Bhabha.
62. Again, recollecting Plato.
63. Although Baugh has no such poem in this collection, the first 'birthing' had begun with the Spanish colonization. However, the Afro-European (English) 'birth' is the most phenomenal.

bay" on its way out of town before "first light" of day. These were the early days of the persona's life, as the boyhood image suggests—the persona being now fully grown into manhood.

The sea has geographical, historical, and personal significance. The sea is a privileged landscape in several ways. Firstly, it is the 'nest' of the Caribbean islands, providing a collective identity. As well, it supports multiple industries—one such vehicle, the "ship", is a recurring image used by Baugh. Like Benítez-Rojo[64], Baugh "repeats" the history of the Trans-Atlantic Slave Trade (again a shipping enterprise). But, more personally, we hear the voice of a youth growing up by the sea. The sea becomes a metaphor for memory—of family life, bonding, pleasure, and a respect for nature. In addition, since the persona "dream[s] on the cobalt sea", the sea occupies a homely space in the persona's consciousness—providing psychic ease.

The other idea of travel—different from physical growth and socio-economic evolution—is of a psychological nature. The speaker indicates in "Small-Town Story" that there is also psychological evolution. The narrator sets the stage when he says that it was a "stagnant town" in which life revolved around "the ships [that] came in [and] went out". Again, there is a sense of one in self imposed 'exile'. On his return he realizes that despite his knowledge of "books and rhetoric" there are no "words" to describe his "disenchant[ment]" with what now stands as a relic of the past—including former "mates". Indeed, the town now really stands as a "Small-Town" "That Had Known Better Days". This idea of psychological evolution is evident in the change in perspective of the narrator in remembering the distant past. The idea of social superiority justifies the celebratory image of the "wedding-feast" in "Small-Town Story". The groom pronounces a clear and superior distinction between his choice of bride and those "plain, fat wom[e]n" of the "Small-Town" whom his former friends now seem to endlessly "grieve". These men of former days were never able to realize their dreams, never able to emerge from the cocoon of false hopes and dreams. They gave themselves to "booze and boorishness" and reaped the consequences. Thus, the persona not only presents himself in juxtaposition with his former mates and outshines them; he presents himself as an example by which the 'others' are measured. Reflecting on the Caribbean experience of personal evolution, it can be seen that many persons have emerged from the simple folk existence

64. *The Repeating Island*

to the benefit of greater intellectual experience and find themselves unable to identify with their past lives. This evolution of life, as in "Small Town . . .", can create a sense of displacement which can happen when someone achieves a new 'identity'. The situation can also be interpreted as a parallel between personal and communal history, and the privileged "I" versus "they" becomes representative.

Another memorable perspective on folklife is presented in the view of the supernatural. This supernatural component which generates fear and awe by its mode and content of delivery can be understood through the image of the prophetess in "The Warner Woman"(109). The Warner-Woman is associated with divinity. She speaks on behalf of another—under the inspiration of a Supreme force—translated from ordinary to extraordinary as a vessel of the supernatural. "The Warner-Woman" remembers a particular era in Caribbean culture when the spirit-possessed woman would walk the streets of the villages and small country towns while making her proclamation. This is a feature of Diaspora culture, and in Chinua Achebe's *Things Fall Apart* we see this Priestess as an integral aspect of West African culture. She is respected and revered—generating both fear and awe in many. Anderson discusses the power of narration—its ability to create a memory of things lost or forgotten—a means, also, of preserving culture. In this particular poem, the "Warner-Woman" is depicted as an awe inspiring performer through whom a new generation receives knowledge of a specific aspect of folk culture, especially significant in that this mode of "warn[ing]" is very near extinction in Jamaica's contemporary culture. While no distinct sense of longing or nostalgia evolves, there is a sense of awe which accompanies the narration.

Again, we can differentiate voices in the narratives. The personal, more intimate voice speaks in "Responsibility" and "The Warner Woman" yet the tones are not the same. The tone in "The Warner Woman" begins with initial imagery of cosiness and comfort—more like that of "Responsibility"—then it bursts into sudden excitement. Words such as "broke . . . / Bell-mouthed and . . . / trumpeted" capture the suddenness in the disruption of peace. Imagine an unexpected clash of cymbals in a musical composition, then things return to normal—is the manner in which this narrative 'performs'—the manner of the "Warner Woman's" burst on the scene.

Ideas concerning the dynamism of the human spirit exude from the poem, "It Was the Singing" (83). The narrative voice is that of a woman, as adamant (in reflecting) as it is jubilant that "it was the singing" that brought her to the moment of spiritual liberation, acceptance of death, and hope in the afterlife. The persona says: ". . . it was only when we raise / "'How Great Thou Art'" that I really feel / the sadness and the glory, wave after wave". This moment is best described as epiphany—working as catalyst to set many visionary and physiological processes into action. The speech act is an apt illustration of the idea of remembrance as muse. The narrator in Zakes Mda's *Ways of Dying* (1991) describes a similar prolific experience:

> Then Noria sang. Jwara found himself overwhelmed by a great creative urge. He took an idle piece of iron, and put it in the fire. When it was red hot, he began to shape it into a strange figure. He amazed himself, because in all his life he had never known that he had such great talent. (30)

The persona in "It Was the Singing" says: "Daddy Walters draw a bass from somewhere / we never hear him go before, and Masie / lift a descant and nobody ask her". We are reminded here of the intertextuality of texts—how they relate to each other—and that also "for some writers, indeed the work of art is its own subject, and tells about itself and the processes whereby it came into being" (Rohlehr 1).

The effect of the singing on the imagination enforced forgiveness and healing. The speaker says that she found it "in [her] heart to forgive"; the singing evoked a spiritual awakening that was "greater / than the paper money overflowing the collection / plate". It worked as a uniting force, binding the community of worshippers—making them "people / together".

The diction of the rendition depicts an individual moving along the "continuum" described by Rohlehr. The language is an attempt to speak the standard English, but it is punctuated with a 'stubborn' vernacular. For example, she says: "It was then I know we was people . . ." and the effort 'betrays' the knowledge that her life is deeply rooted in the folk experience.

The individual subjective consciousness is made to represent the collective consciousness. Not only in the foregoing poem, but also in many of the poems in this collection is a narrative of a common human experience that makes the stories relevant and of extra-textual value.

CRITICAL THINKING

3. In what respect does "River Song" (48) depict folklife? What can you deduce from the nuance "surprised by love"? How can you justify your conclusion with evidence in the poem?

4. What of memory does the speaker evoke in "Memories Like Comfort Stones" (45)? How can you make a comparable analysis with "Black Sand" (16)?

Narratives on Nature, or Memories of a Romantic Sensibility

Baugh crafts many poems in a personal, intimate, narrative style—where seemingly, the reader is being lured into the imagination of the narrator. Also, in these poems, the persona's voice is strongly characterized so that the sense of 'I am speaking to you' is clearly communicated. This sense of invitation into 'partnership' which is evoked by the voice distinctly heightens appreciation of the subject matter.

It is undisputable that the imagination is fundamental for the creation of poetry. Perhaps it is a literary phenomenon of the 1780s, or just plain uncanny that this period 'birthed' a cadre of poets classified as the Romantics,[65] who collectively are responsible for a long lasting celebratory period of poetic imagination. As in other cultural awakenings, the Romantic movement has its devotees—we find the reminiscence of the Romantic imagination in specific works of Baugh which appeal to the reader's imagination even when they suggest autobiographic contexts. The Romantics privilege the spiritual component of human nature and also the beauty and wonder of physical nature. Some of Baugh's poems evoke ideas of human nature, as well as, human interaction with nature and these contexts become 'sites' for imaginative exploration.

One poem which highlights a Romanticized attitude to the past very well is "Sunday Afternoon Walks with My Father" (67). This poem evokes a voice of reverence and awe, encapsulated within a bonding leisurely walk to the quayside. In the first verse the persona comments on the "cathedral quiet / . . . [and] white breasted devotions of pigeons" which suggest a kind of worshipful respect for the occasion. The ceremonial evocation enlarges as the "old bosun shuffled down from his stool"—suggesting haste in his actions—to "usher [them] through the wicket gate". Later on the speaker tells us that he enters "a side chapel [he] had not entered before". The image of bonding is complete as the persona explains that he "walked whisperingly [with his hand] in [his] father's" and we also get the sense of cooperative communal closeness with other members of the community.

Imagery of physical nature is profuse in Baugh's poetry. For instance,

65. Namely, William Blake, George Gordon Lord Byron, Samuel Taylor Coleridge, John Keats, Percy Bysshe Shelley, William Wordsworth.

in "Long Service Award" (79), in spite of the obvious marginalization suffered by the woman, as "she leans on the window-sill looking out / . . . she sees shooting stars falling down / the bright November sky . . . / [and] the greatness of the world move in her". Her sense of suffering fades out as the illuminating light of the cosmos affect her imagination. In these words the speaker shows that the woman is in a transcendental mode of worship which is revelatory. Though her physical circumstance remains unchanged, her spiritual being is connected to a greater force which 'improves' her condition.

In "Visiting Professor" (87) the speaker says: "But draw back the curtains. Look.", in a dramatic mode. Having gained his imaginary audience's attention, he continues: "The blanketed horses are grazing / on the lower slopes as if exactly / as I last saw them at nightfall". Why should an apparently ordinary event take on extraordinary significance? To an ordinary viewer it would seem commonplace, nonetheless, the romantic observer will invoke particular significance. And, in the midst of this 'spectacle', the speaker acknowledges "a rosella [which] enhances the morning".

There are two particular poems which suggest a kind of tease on the imaginative processes: "Hedge Trimming" (88) and "A Tale from the Rainforest" (107). Although the first line in "Hedge Trimming" at first appears to echo Walcott's *Another Life*—which it may well do—it is worthwhile to give careful consideration to the idea that Walcott's poem is primarily a vision of another life lived in the flesh. In "Hedge Trimming" there is the suggestion of reincarnation—a spiritual transformation into a new being. The reference to Blake reinstates Baugh as a protégé of the Romantic poets. The idea of spiritual transformation is solidified in the last three lines: "Neighbourhood dogs will take back to their mistresses' / drawing rooms reports of strange sightings: / a wild man laughing through the undergrowth". These words evoke an image of the supernatural and a persona who imagines himself 'free'.

"A Tale from the Rainforest" could be interpreted as symbolic of the need for spiritual rest or ease for the imagination. The bird says: "[t]he grief of the rainforest / is sometimes hard to bear"—contrasting with the positive image associated with rainforest. "Grief" could, therefore, be interpreted to mean a condition of being overwhelmed and the need for respite. During respite, the mind and imagination are refreshed, creating fertile ground for creativity. Such is the image in "[t]hey made music / together". However, the relief is only temporary as "the rivermaid called time / and the nameless bird / flew back to the rainforest". The foregoing poems appeal to the imagination in depicting nature as the primary source of meaning.

Critical Thinking

5. What is the mood in "I wish you A Leaf Falling" (44)? Analyse the appeal (of imagery) on the imagination.

6. Write a critical appreciation of "Slight and Ornamental" (25) in which you prove that the poem "celebrates a bond between nature and the human mind".

Facets of Postcolonial Memory, or Memories of the Collective Historical Consciousness of the Caribbean

Narration of Afro-Caribbean experience in literary form by Caribbean writers possibly began with the awareness of nationalism and subsequent and growing discomfort with colonial models[66]. A specific date concerning the very first creative (Caribbean) publication is difficult to ascertain. Bruce King (1979) records that West Indian literature 'emerged' after World War 2 and publications are recorded from the eighteenth-century onwards. He continues in saying that this earlier literature reflects growing nationalism and feelings of anticolonialism. Also, in addition to the discomfort with colonial literary models that King asserts, certainly, after emancipation and the growing opportunities for intellectual development of the Afro-Caribbean, many writers had the opportunity to develop their talents. Having 'rejected' that which is associated with the slave master's culture, a literature which would express their own sense of self and cultural experience became necessary. Thus, they sought to establish their own sense of place and space.[67] The problem with place arises out of the displacement of Africans caused by the Trans-Atlantic Slave Trade, while space is dependent on whether or not this need for the knowledge and acceptance of self, and a sense of rootedness is satisfied. The circumstances of African displacement—colonialism and enslavement—and the Afro-Caribbean's need for self-worth and equality with the oppressor are depicted in the works of Caribbean poets, including Baugh. Whether consciously or unconsciously, this urge for expression evolved into what is now described as Caribbean literature.

In Caribbean literature the topos of memory is multifaceted[68] as well as polemic[69]. Baugh represents memory often (but not always) depicted through the narratives[70] of the simple folk—a depiction with inherent complexities[71]. These creative inventions (in poetry) have an ultimate

66. I draw this conclusion after a study of Laurence Breiner's *An Introduction to West Indian Poetry* (1998). This observation is also supported in *West Indian Literature* (1979), ed. Bruce King.
67. Brathwaite's personae in "Tom" and "Folkways" in *The Arrivants* (1973) depict this need of the African in the New World.
68. As examples, are folk memory, body memory, autobiographic memory.
69. Walcott's "The Muse of History", for example, encourages debate.
70. That is, "its foregrounding of a series of events or actions which are connected in time" (Bennett and Royle 55).
71. More fully developed in "Narratives of Folklife".

purpose which is to convey a larger truth or greater understanding beyond what their formal appearances suggest. By crafting these events through the lifestyles, beliefs and customs of ordinary people (simple folk) the 'tale' appears deceptively harmless. However, within the structure of the story, are metaphoric representations—hidden truths—which are often culturally specific. Since narrative is partly the medium through which history is recorded, it is possible to understand how Anderson's theory of narrating events into the minds of a new generation has relevance. This, of course, originates in the ancient practice where storytelling, and not writing, was the chief function of storing cultural values. Many of Baugh's poems are created in narrative style, and even though they do not all tell their 'tale' in the same manner, in these poems are ideas of marginality and displacement, oppression, violence, and ambivalence.

An outstanding poem in the collection, *Black Sand,* depicting Caribbean postcolonial history is, "Sometimes in the Middle of the Story" (128). This poem is the "Story" (literary re-creation) or narration of the African's journey through the Middle Passage. It stands as an artistic naming, as well as, a performance which is a strategy for memory creation. That is, the story is crafted in narrative 'time' and functions as a memorial. It then becomes a method of teaching history to a new generation.

This poem—"Sometimes in the Middle of the Story"—salutes ancestral struggles and celebrates triumph over adversity. The particular reference to "Toussaint . . . moving / faster than backra-massa timepiece / know to measure", is a succinct expression of skilful manoeuvre employed in eluding colonial powers. The words "strategy" and "trap" draw on military operations against the enemy. The idea behind the fights and struggles is to end the "shuttle" of human cargo through the "paths of ocean". Participating in the speech act is a small gathering representing a generation waiting for the knowledge of their roots and the reason for their presence in the New World—"the children". The poem also provides substantive evidence for Anderson's theory of re-living an experience through narration,[72] and also that of the act of narration which provides memory essential for the understanding of one's identity.

72. This aspect concerns "Memory and Forgetting" and in particular "The Biography of Nations" (187+)

The title of the poem is instructive in its ambiguity. The word "Middle" is a reminder of the route taken by slave ships from West Africa through the Atlantic to the Americas and back. "Middle" is a lasting reminder, a kind of mnemonical cue for the re-call of what Benítez-Rojo describes as the act of "Europe conceiv[ing] the project of inseminating the Caribbean womb with the blood of Africa" (5)—an unpleasant reminder of the "Middle Passage". "Middle" draws also on the idea of the interrupted existence of mainly West African peoples, and spans a period of history widely known as a period of enslavement of black people—a time between the official beginning and ending of that experience. "Middle" also evokes the idea of ambivalence—a period of limbo when identity is in a crisis. But, "Middle" becomes self-reflexive as it registers, also, the interrupted portion of the speech act—the "Story" being told. We do not have a clear indication of what the first "Story"—the main narrative—is. But, relying on knowledge of the oral tradition, this is a significant moment of recreation or strategic storytelling. This middle narrative supersedes the original "Story", taking precedence over it. The indication is unmistakable: we need to pay attention, think on, remember, our collective history, "Sometimes", and this colonial history is at the nexus of Caribbean culture. The context of this poem is 'old' but here we see it 'new' in mythical or re-created artistic form as an event of memory.

Additionally, "Sometimes in the Middle of the Story" celebrates ancestral lineage and the indomitable spirit of "drowned Africans" whose "souls shuttle / still the forest paths of ocean / connecting us still". The idea of the everlasting, enduring spirit of the African is depicted in the imagery of ancestral connection in the Caribbean.

Meanwhile, the interior monologue, "Nigger Sweat" (126), is as harsh as it is desperate in its postcoloniality. Eliciting grim humour, demonstrating cynical behaviour, barely suppressed anger, and desperation on the part of the persona, "Nigger Sweat" depicts an ironic twist on the black man's quest for revenge by locating refuge in the land of the oppressor. A journey-through-history motif is sustained in linking "Sometimes in the Middle of the Story" with "Nigger Sweat". The word, "Nigger", is the derogatory naming of the black (African) man and it becomes a new name for (in this case) a man who has been robbed of his respectability and the right to pursue, freely, a life suitable to himself and others. The idea of "Sweat" is significantly naming a physiological release from toil but it is echoing degradation, discrimination, and the exploitation of the "slave holding plantation" and the "febrile" labour of the enslaved negroes (Benítez-Rojo 5). More immediate is the speaker's own "sweat[ing]" and the sense of stress and urgency he feels from the burden imposed on him by the authorities. Any dignified life of the negro is proscribed after his capture, landing and enslaved existence, and his 'new' life is an antithesis of the 'old'.[73] This persona—a negro—portrays no sense of valued history and this vacuum is filled with anger and "remorse". Thus, the speaker in "Nigger Sweat" narrates not only his sense of personal history, but also, a collective history, and finds himself in an emotional whirlwind of ambivalence, vengeance and irony as he seeks escape into further oppression.

The narrative constructs so far observed (re-created as poetry) is a strategy used to prevent, in this Afro-Caribbean context, a certain "amnesia" (Anderson 204) and is perpetuated through the oral tradition, as well as, through literary means. In the sense of the literary, we see a highly selective characterization in a situation where issues emerge. The issues are told, not in the formal teller-audience setting, but in a reconstituted reality—a necessary invention. But, even in the oral tradition—where stories are told by word of mouth—invention is often done. In the case of "Nigger Sweat" though, the suppressed narratives relate to lived events in Jamaica's (and Caribbean) history. The persona in "Nigger Sweat" is yearning "to find a little life" in order to subvert the stereotypical image associated with "black people". This quest for self-knowledge and personal value means that what "can not be 'remembered', must be narrated" (Anderson 204). "Nigger Sweat" functions as a double narrative, juxtaposing colonial ('old') alongside black ('new') history in the Caribbean.

Again, the journey motif re-emerges. It is near impossible to escape "this river running through history" (126) when collective history is examined. "Nigger Sweat" is a poignant deconstruction of psychic (dis)ease—a condition emerging out of searching for a sense of self and worthiness amidst neocolonialism. The "Nigger" in The New World must find a sense of belonging, wealth, and prosper in wealth, to authenticate his humanity and restore his pride. As well, the

73. Anderson's theory speaks of a 'new' named after the 'old' in the new community formed, but Africans in The New World by reason of enslavement are not privileged in this theory. The negativity attached to this 'new' existence I view as an antithesis of Anderson's theory.

"Story" of our ancestors must be told—narrated into the memory of a new generation—if only to provide a sense of understanding. More importantly, it must be told to increase the value of our ancestral struggles and present culture. When these criteria have been in some measure achieved, it is then that the moment for the exploration of our personal histories—our autobiographic experience—becomes plausible. The tendency of a people to narrate their history will always inspire creative minds to re-create it, and Baugh's particularly humorous, ironic, dramatic narrative style characterize the foregoing poems.

It appears that where the collective history is particularly burdensome or involves unfortunate circumstances,[74] the greater the need to preserve the memory. This is apparent in the case of displacement or marginalization of Africans by the slave trade. Occasionally, the history of that past is altered or distorted, or constructed (invented memory) as mythical. Some of our postcolonial writers throughout the diaspora—peoples of "colonial displacement" (Ashcroft, Griffiths and Tiffin 217)—reconstruct this memory so that the work evokes anger, sadness or guilt[75]. Though it can be seen that this memory is sometimes burdensome,[76] Baugh tempers these poems with varying degrees of humour or hopefulness.

It is feasible to argue that there is an urge to memorialize that which is valued for its beauty or impact on the mind. In Afro-Caribbean history the memory of enslavement is negative or unpleasant. Yet, this facet of memory is necessary for the validation of (dis)placement and the construction of identity that is critical in understanding and accepting Afro-Caribbean presence in the New World. When Baugh constructs, for example, "Sometimes in the Middle of the Story", he constructs the collective identity of the Caribbean region. His work, in this aspect, is related to the work of other Caribbean literary writers, including those who create prose and drama. This reinforces the words of Michel Foucault[77] when he states: "The frontiers of a [work] . . . is caught up in a system of references to other [works], other texts, other sentences: it is a node within a network" (423). Baugh's poetry fit into what is perceived as a Caribbean canon. There is an historical network of Afro-Caribbean people linked by the common experience,

74. (such as the story of ancient Israel in Egypt and their deliverance)
75. An evocation which Walcott engages with in the "Muse of History".
76. For example, in "Long Service Award" and "Nigger Sweat"
77. In *The Archaeology of Knowledge reprinted in Literary Theory: An Anthology* (2003).

common memory, of enslavement, and there are writers who respond to their interaction with this knowledge, variously. Moreover, Mikhail Bakhtin also voices the phenomenon of the collective authorial network in saying that "no living word relates to its object in a *singular* way: between the word and its object, between the word and the speaking subject, there exists . . . the same theme . . ." (276). That is an acceptable argument concerning how the singular experience is also related to the collective. Each word used as language to express has a related experience. Walcott, as a Caribbean writer, theorizes and demonstrates perhaps a defiant preference for an alternative to evoking the victimization related to colonialism, but Baugh's work demonstrates that collective memory has its place. The foregoing poems depict collective memory in the topos of colonization and the effects of enslavement. The more pleasant experience of the simple folk tradition is otherwise discussed.

MARGINALITY OR DISPLACEMENT

One concern for discussion that has colonialism as its matrix is marginality or displacement. Marginalization can occur through an oppressive situation that causes an individual or individuals to be regarded as 'an other'—meaning discriminated against, in its broadest concept, or narrowly, non white. Those who represent the colonial power or ruling class set themselves up as superior while 'the others' are inferior. However, marginalization can be observed or experienced in any situation where a person does not, due to the circumstance, feel a sense of worthiness and belonging or suffers from a feeling of inequality. In addition to "Nigger Sweat" (previously discussed), there are several poems which depict marginality or displacement.

For instance, the poem "Long Service Award" (79) is prefaced by a quotation that is an unmistakable reminder of the black man's life in the slaveholding plantation. The quoted planter is reflective, and there is irony in his observation: a human who is worked as an animal ought to find labour "repugnant"[78]. The poem is addressing ethnic issues, exploitation, and marginality. The essence of the poem, however, is the re-creation of memory.

78. This is a 1776 quotation by Edward Long, a planter.

The persona in "Long Service Award" suffers the pain of exploitation because the length of service or time for which she is supposed to be awarded is mocked by the gift of a clock. The "clock" is the new representation of the old—named as "Long Service Award" (symbolic of a time of service). The value of the service is down played, firstly, by the blind indifference to her needs, and secondly, by the 'devalued' gift of a clock. Her master is colonial—white—while she is black. The depth and hardship of her labour are sensed by the description of the "big boss'" hands being "so pink and soft . . . / than a white baby's bottom, or the just born mice". In stark contrast with "the man's hands", this woman's hands have spent "fifty years traversing the cane / back bent, beaten by sun and rain". The severe hardship of her life has prevented her from birthing and raising a healthy child so that she has only an "invalid daughter" who can provide no tangible relief to her in her old age. This woman has spent her life living on the periphery called otherness, and has grown to accept her fate despite her awareness of servitude—a situation that the speaker in "Nigger Sweat" defies. As the persona reflects on the occasion and value of her award, a sense of smouldering bitterness is in her tone as she says: "But really, it isn't strange, it's only / salt rubbed slowly into the wound of time". Does not the time-piece which is her gift bear witness? "Long Service Award" is then an ironic presentation of a reward for long term value.

There exists a similarity in the ironic twist of "Long Service Award" and that of "The Carpenter's Complaint" (120). The persona in "The Carpenter's Complaint" is vexed due to the manner in which he sees himself being 'awarded' for the years of long service to his close friend, now deceased. A friendship once valued is now seen as completely devalued, and with it, the speaker's own sense of personal value. The quest for the knowledge of self runs parallel to the increase in the value of selfhood. The narrators in "Long Service Award" and "The Carpenter's Complaint" have both arrived at a point in their life journey when their sense of personal value was expected to be affirmed. This was their 'incremental' moment. Yet, they were both 'rewarded' with disappointment and left with a sense of betrayal of loyalty toward those responsible for affirming their sense of worth.

"The Carpenter's Complaint" is a dramatic monologue depicting one persona's sense of violation of personal value. The speaker is seeking to regain his sense of importance. He takes this moment on 'centre stage' to deconstruct the negative image he construes and reconstructs a positive or more acceptable image through remembrance. However, the persona in "Long Service Award" finds solace in the "greatness" of nature and in the thought of a more powerful Being in existence.

Indeed, the persona in "The Carpenter's Complaint" heightens his sense of value and re-positions himself by contrastingly devaluing all others who stand in opposition. The deceased man's son is a "mawga-foot bwoy" and the man who gets the job instead is a "big-belly crook who don't know him arse / from a chisel". The "university" which is usually respected as a place of higher learning is now an institution that re-makes individuals into "fool[s]". Thus, the speaker deploys a strategy for self preservation. "The Carpenter's Complaint" gives a bitter-sweet performance of self restoration from margin to centre, tempered with humorous outrage.

On the other hand, the sense of displacement is subtle in "Visiting Professor" (87). It is masked by the shifting consciousness of the persona who is engaged in an interior monologue. The sense of urgency toward the end of the first verse is displaced by the immediacy of awareness of setting, which interferes with what the persona is essaying to get done—write a paper. But, the sense of longing for home coupled with the uncertainty concerning the reception of the paper, distracts the persona. There is a gentle humour that is evoked from the sense of the persona apparently talking with himself that the 'conversation' demonstrates—inviting the reader who also participates as audience. The sense of urgency is underscored by the repetitive lines: "[t]his place is called . . ." and the double message in the urge to "get back to the paper" is as well, get back "home", and get back to belongingness. The memory of home performs as interference in this particular poem, and underscores the need for belonging as essential for productivity.

The feeling of displacement has produced the kind of mental inertia that the persona experiences toward the writing task. But, interestingly, the interior monologue reveals a volatile imagination at work. The persona's thoughts move fluidly from one subject matter to another—remembering one thing or the other. At the end of the second verse we get the answer to the problem: "marginalia". "Marginalia" is the "draw back", and we get the pun in "draw back the curtains", to mean, "[l]ook" back (or remember) "colonial" times.

Accordingly, the persona subsequently identifies the root of the sense of "marginalia" being experienced, in the lines: "I have counted my footfalls echoing down post- / colonial corridors". The 'new' naming of the corridors re-calls the memory of colonialism, but it is just as significant to note the sense of difference that this particular memory evokes.

Truly, the memory of European exploitation is an extremely important one in the Caribbean experience. Caribbean literary artists choose to remember it in varied contexts. Whether or not such actions imply servitude[79] to the colonial past, is contingent upon how our collective history—postcolonial history—is perceived to impact on the present generation.

These poems are examples of narratives, but their strategies are not all the same. For example, their "logical or causal connections" (Bennett and Royle 56) vary. "Sometimes in the Middle of the Story" has the voice of the omniscient narrator. This narrator stands at a certain 'distance' from the events and his voice is the voice of wisdom and instruction. He knows that what "move[s] outside the house" is "not the wind". However, he constructs a myth to provide the answer—employing invention to arrive at truth. What is the truth? It is not that a ghost just rode past. The truth lies in the reasons for the "Africans [in the] Middle Passage"—it answers why there is African presence in the Caribbean and the long lasting effect and significance of related events. Notwithstanding, the story ends on a positive note, empowering "black men" in their struggles.

A similar narrative voice is perceived in "Long Service Award", which, despite the foregrounding of the awardee's discomfiture, ends with the woman humbly resigned. Is the voice of the narrator implying, by this, the need to accept what we cannot change? Or does it empower the woman in some way to displace her 'oppressor' by shifting her memory of "Service" and focusing instead on the "shooting stars . . . / the bright November sky . . . [and] / the greatness of the world"? Here we see a shifting of power as a "strategy for the weak and dispossessed" (Bennett and Royle 60), so that the woman emerges somewhat empowered.

A more forceful and personal narrative voice is evident in "Nigger Sweat", as well as, "The Carpenter's Complaint". As dramatic monologues, the stories narrate critical moments in which

79. Alluding here to Derek Walcott's "The Muse of History"

the speakers negotiate or seek to re-claim personal identities. The direct sense of involvement of the audience invites different responses, however. "Nigger Sweat" evokes issues related to collective history, while "The Carpenter's Complaint" reveals the attitude of an individual toward a personal relationship. But, they both end in dissatisfaction—not satisfying the usual expectation of closure. Thus, these narratives are narratives that call for action as they disrupt structural 'norms'.

Lastly, "Visiting Professor" is fascinating for its deceptive anti-narrative construction. Its internal contradictions (continuous digressions), rather than disturb the 'tale', subtly incorporate multiple narratives which, due to partial disclosures, draw the reader more powerfully into the relationship established with the narrator. The figure represented in "Visiting Professor" is, in contrast with the foregoing poems, not a folk figure, and its rhetorical style is parallel to its subject matter. This narrative is more lyrical in nature[80] due to its narrative point of view and preoccupation with a particular state of mind.

Yet, in all, the topos of memory is distinctive. These poems depict postcoloniality despite their different settings and characterization, and exemplify re-constructions of memory. While some facets are based on actual or factual collective history, others are crafted as mythical constructs. In the end, the objective is that of the reconstitution of a reality to portray a certain 'truth'.

Critical Thinking

7. a. Read the poem, "To the Editor Who Asked Me to Send Him Some of My Black Poems" (27).

   b. What aspects of Baugh's poetic style are evident?

8. What thematic comparison can be made between "A Nineteenth -Century Portrait" (28) and the other poems in this section?

80. Imaginative, gently expressive, appealing, thoughtful.

Writing the Nation

When the word 'nation' becomes the focus of our attention, more often than not, what immediately is imagined is a country, a geographical location with its own government. We can accept this, as it is a definition that will be supported by a dictionary at this[81] level. In this context, we can conceptualize Jamaica, being the place of Baugh's birth. It is important to note, however, that the name, Jamaica, does not appear in any poem in the collection, *Black Sand.* In what respect, then, can it be said that Baugh writes the nation? How can this be proved?

If persons were to mask their physical appearance completely, there is still something about them that would enable us to establish a particular identity, or by which they are able to depict a certain identity, and that is through the spoken word.[82] This is not just possible to be analysed in Baugh's poetry, but in the genres of literature, whether printed or dramatized. When writers create characters who are language oriented, they are seeking to communicate more than mere characterization, for in this technique many ideologies are frequently embodied.

One very exemplary poem that evokes nation is "The Carpenter's Complaint" (120). "The Carpenter's Complaint"[83] is a stirring performance of a man who is hurting acutely, and who has the need to testify of the deeds that validate his call for justice. The poem is crafted in a diction that merges the standard with the vernacular, and its Jamaicanness is depicted by the creole (patois) that punctuate the tale—the mannerisms of the speaker. The characterization of nation is authenticated—made real—when the speaker says in indignation: "Damn mawga-foot bwoy . . . him give it to *Mister* Belnavis to make—/ . . . fi-him coffin must better / than mine!" One can get a sense of strained effort to speak 'proper' English, as "better / than mine" can be understood as 'betta / than fi-mi' in the full vernacular, but Baugh crafts just enough to evoke a sensibility in contrast with the "university" persona quietly depicted. Voice plays a central role in this reading, but it does not preclude the theme of marginalization. As a work of art, such a poem is then transportable, and wherever in the world it is read or contemplated, Jamaica as nation is "exhibit[ed]".[84]

81. Advanced, or college (such as the *Concise Oxford English Dictionary*, eleventh edition)
82. (With the exception of the dumb, of course.)
83. Also discussed on pages 18 and 49
84. Benítez-Rojo

Another poem that evokes a Jamaican ethos is "Nigger Sweat" (126). In this poem[85] the speaker is carrying out a conversation in his head. We can know that it is in his head because some aspects of the conversation are threatening and the persona is in a situation in which he is under surveillance and is clearly "sweat[ing]" from uneasiness. He knows that he is at the mercy of the interviewer, and so is making effort to calm himself and clear his "sweat[ing]" face with his "handkerchief". Notwithstanding, he cannot help complaining that ". . . the cool-cut, crew-cut Marine boy / wid him ice-blue eye and / walkie-talkie dissa walk through the place and pretend / him no see we". More specifically, "wid him" and "dissa walk" voice a legitimate Jamaican consciousness. Comparably, in "The Town That Had Known Better Days" (69) we get an account of a fight which is "badder than those . . . at the town's / one cinema" between two girls over a sailor. In the foregoing examples, are how Baugh depicts a nation without boundary, and legitimizes nation as a "principle".[86]

Another respect in which Baugh writes the nation is more conventional in the understanding of nation. This falls into the first context of nation introduced. This concept is also evoked in "Nigger Sweat". The heading of the poem locates the context as "Kingston, 1982" which speaks for itself, being the capital of Jamaica. Other poems have names of geographical sites. For example, "View from the George Headley Stand, Sabina" (80) readily evokes a narrative of Jamaica's sport history and one of its landmarks. In "The Town That Had Known Better Days" we read of "raftsmen spurring / their bamboo horses down the Rio Grande"—a river in Portland, one of Jamaica's eastern parishes. This is the same river alluded to in "Choices" (58) when the speaker says: "River mullet still running in Grandy water". This is a river that attracts tourists to the pleasure of "raft[ing]". Port Antonio, though not named, is a "picturesque, ramshackle port" which is a "haven" for tourists, as well as, a busy socioeconomic trade centre. Also, Baugh's renowned "The Warner Woman" (109) depicts an aspect of Jamaica's seventeenth-century history in the name "Port Royal".[87] It is not just the shipping and commercial extravaganza of the era that are evoked, but also, the historic 1692 earthquake[88] that buried more than half of the city and its treasures, and the notoriety of pirates that make the

85. Also discussed on page 45
86. Validating Ernest Renan
87. Also discussed on page 35
88. The first of several recorded disasters.

city legendary. Baugh merges two legendary icons—of the spiritual and the geographical—to create an artefact of the nation in "The Warner Woman".

According to Ernest Renan (1882), the effort to define nation is susceptible to "dangerous misunderstandings". This is partly because of the implications of a strictly geographical understanding. However, when we can imagine collective ethos—a kind of psychosocial phenomenon that emerges from the melting pot of language, religion, ethnicity, food, physical and political environment which is dynamic and transportable—it is agreeable that a nation is greater than any boundary. So long as that ethos remains, successive generations will inherit this consciousness which sets them apart. It is then possible to see how Jamaica can exist in another part of the world even though the land mass is fixed in the Caribbean Sea. Antonio Benítez-Rojo encourages the thought that literature is not to be seen as "quiet and private as prayer"(22) as such a work of art has limitless (worldwide) possibilities. Writing the nation, then, is more than naming geographical sites, for wherever the work is "exhibit[ed]"(23), a nation can be depicted through mannerisms, site references and cultural norms.

Critical Thinking

9. How is nation depicted in the following poems:

    a. "Joe Waugh, Engine Driver" (66)?

    b. "Lignum Vitae" (129)?

    c. "Memories Like Comfort Stones" (45)?

10. What nations are depicted in "The Accident" (19) and "Walking to Jerusalem" (39)? You can figure out the answers by studying the speech patterns.

Ideas of Death

One of the benefits derived from the study of literature is the acquisition of communicative skills. It is not only that a wide study of creative writings expose us to an inexhaustible reservoir of figurative language, it is also that we become increasingly motivated to use them in our speech and writings. This is due to the infectious nature of creative expressions, and also that the more we become immersed in it, is the more we are able to recognize and 'decipher' their nuances. At first glance, many of the poems in this category may appear somewhat indefinable, but the figurative language is so crafty that the poems repay careful and close analyses. This section will explore images of death—some subtle, others striking.

Subtle Death

The first (and very short) poem in this collection—"End Poem"—sets the tone for the depictions of death which can be found in the "New Poems"[89]. "End Poem" speaks of the imminent fall of a "song tower" and the wish or expectation that "goats and children" will find "delight" in rummaging in its ruins. The image of indulgence is extended to nature where the effervescent gleam of sunlight is expected to brighten the ruins and heighten the senses of those among its degenerative rubble.

The image in this deceptively simple poem is interesting and complex. Since concrete has no life to sing, this "song tower" is a metaphoric representation of a person (songs being a literary representation of verses) and this person has a reservoir of verses—a writer of verses, and we know that such persons are called poets. The "fall", then, is the physical demise of the writer—death. While the idea of a graveyard is not farfetched, notice that the disintegrated relics are not buried from view, but are accessible.

A deeper analysis of the image of "daring song-tower" not only suggests strength, but also impact and force that can be attributed to the persona who is at this moment of 'singing', being creative. Desire is subsequently evoked through "may goats and children know delight", and this desire is for the persona—more than the work itself—to eclipse the darkness or extinction that not only burial[90] is likely to bring, but if the persona were to be uncelebrated. The tone in which death is being

89. Which are conveniently grouped with respect to their period of publication. The theme of ideas of death is being dealt with in this regard to the time of publication only.
90. Both literal and figurative in depiction.

contemplated is mild, seeing that it is complemented with bright and happy imagery of nature, but there is irony deep within. For, while death is accepted as inevitable, its finality is shunned.

An image of sustainability is projected toward succeeding generations, as is depicted in "children" who are usually 'fed' on a diet of verses in their early years, and since the animals are "goats" a lot can be also conceived. Firstly, why "goat" and not sheep? Maybe it's simply the natural tendencies between the two with respect to breeding—goats in some context may rummage more than sheep. Where ruins are concerned, the idea of surefootedness belongs to the goat. But, we can also think of the negative 'goat' versus the positive 'sheep' in alluding to human tendencies and behaviour. In this context, the persona expresses the desire that the "songs" may affect even "goats"—unlikely lovers of verses—and that impact would be significant, indeed.

We can, therefore, consider a Romantic imagination at work when the image of "sunlight" glorifies the scene. Even though time will inevitably make its mark of even partial obscurity as seen in the image of "weed-grown walls", the light eclipses such sign of decadence. The irony suggested between the title and the poem is that the end is desired to be symbolic of a beginning or a continuation of life in a more or less profound way, and it is also noteworthy to say that the desire for perpetuation is a common human tendency.

A subtle image of death is evoked, also, in the poem, "Telling the Time" (33) in a rather gentle and humorous note. The poem begins with an identification of the time of day when an "old woman" leaves her "bed" and dresses in her "Sunday clothes" and starts moving about the house. It is not yet dawn and the frightened grand children question her seemingly irrational behaviour, emphasizing that the time for travelling out is wrong. The "old woman" states that a "man / [is] coming to take the house". But, the speaker tells us that already the house is fully owned by the "old woman". The persona then continues explaining that the "old woman" is teaching a lesson (perhaps by instinct rather than awareness) that someone—"a man"—is "always" returning to take back what belongs to him in a timely manner.

The humour in the situation is partly evoked through the dramatic dialogue between the "old woman" and the grand children, and the conflict between the hour of day ("3 a.m.") versus her decision to get dressed for the imminent 'visitor'. Considering the absence of reprimand or ridicule of the "old woman['s]" actions, the mood of the speaker is more indulgent than harsh. The most significant implication of the event is not so much that the "old woman" is losing her faculties, seeing that "the mortgage is discharged", but that she is clairvoyant. For, while the speaker does not mention death in the literal sense, its subtle indication is in the euphemistic allusion to "a man coming to repossess / and he picks his time".

An image of subtle death is also in "Freeze Warning" (34). The captioned lyrics above the poem tell of a "songbird" singing at a "window". In the song is the bird singing at the "window" of the speaker who "wait[s] every day for his voice". The speaker gives the name of the "songbird" as "Heavenly Love" and the name of the song as "Rejoice!". The explanation for the significance of the verse is that it was taught to the speaker by the persona's mother.

The song has some bearing on the poem. The context of the poem is that of the "second . . . day of Spring" and instead of sunny, cool weather, the "day" is not only very cold, but frost is expected later in the night. The speaker is reflecting on his elderly friend—a "poet"—who has sent a new poem to the persona. This poem had been crafted to depict another event of "Spring" in the past, quite unlike the present dubious weather. The persona continues to describe his friend whom he refers to as "old angora" and who is apparently being aroused in some way as he "configures" ideas of sexuality in verses. This, the "poet-friend" confesses, is influenced by "the sickness / of the country . . . the sadness of the land". It is the confession of the "poet-friend" that has evoked the memory of the captioned song the speaker learned from his or her mother. And, so, the "reply" to the friend is the heeding of the instruction at the end of the song—that the "poet-friend" should "Rejoice!".

Both "Telling the Time" (33) and "Freeze Warning" (34) register the human practice of using euphemisms or connotated expressions when speaking of death. The idea that "the man / coming to take the house" and "always a man coming to repossess" are clearly not literal as the speaker says that there is no outstanding "mortgage". Therefore, the search for understanding directs to age-old cultural expressions and figurative allusions to the human body. We can then interpret "house" as body. If the "mortgage" does not exist, neither does "the man"—

which makes "the man" an ideological concept—meaning something without form, being intangible. These ideas are augmented by the title "grandma", signifying old age. We can then make a parallel reading in "Freeze Warning". Firstly, moving above the literal sense in both titles, "Telling the Time" time can then be interpreted as ("Grandma") telling the time of her death, as in knowing that death is imminent. While, in "Freeze Warning" we can go beyond the literal frost and readily consider the condition of being frozen—being lifeless, inactive or dead. Then, "Freeze Warning" is notice of imminent death. Hence, the two titles depict similar ideas in a connotated sense.

Going beyond the title of "Freeze Warning", we can see other nuances of impending death. Firstly, there is also "wait[ing]" and "Heaven" that directs us to think of thoughts projected beyond physical existence. Even though "Heaven" is a popular Christian vision, persons who believe in reincarnation also believe that there must first be death of the person to be reincarnated. Then, there is the image of old age in "old angora" but which evokes the animal instincts of the man, who is defying age due to "testosterone thudding in his balls". This aroused condition of the man, however, becomes ironic and incompatible with his ageing condition. This ironic evocation of "testosterone" also implies a pun on the word "Spring". The "old angora" found his organ 'springing'—and this idea is supported in the depictions of "young girls", "bellying" and "perennial procreation". So, although we see the literal "Winter" manifesting itself into "Spring", in the persona's "old" friend, though he is nearer to death than life, he is 'springing' with the life of a younger man. We are then led away from the initial idea of death, not so much that he should welcome it by "[r]ejoic[ing]", but that he should "[r]ejoice!" in his condition.

CRITICAL THINKING

11. Consider as many of the euphemistic expressions of death used in your culture as you can and write them down. Compare your findings with your classmates to see whether there are more you could learn. Can you figure out the root or origin of each of these terms?

12. How many subtle ideas of death can you figure out in the following poems?

    a. "The Dark Hole in the Garden" (37). To whom does the speaker refer to as "He"? What idea do you get from: "But there's this dark hole in the garden"? How do you substantiate your answer?

    b. "Hedge Trimming" (88). What phrase suggests the idea of reincarnation? Can you tell who the persona is alluding to as "Blake's", and in what context is this reference used?

STARK IMAGERY OF DEATH

While many nuances of death tease the imagination, there are also some sharply clear imagery. One of these is evoked in "The Accident" (19). This poem is about a lawyer who was found dead along a roadway with his brains dashed out of his skull. The speaker tells us that after the body was found a wave of shock rippled through the island. The persona reflects on the dead lawyer's personal and professional attributes and accomplishments, including his "sweet Guyana" wife whose brilliance was noted.

The reflection takes a clairvoyant turn when the speaker starts reporting folk wisdom and insight of the accident. The persona says that persons have a lot to say about the accident and especially what led to it; it happened by divine intervention, or "God". The man "O.C." while living was seen as a man who had no respect for "God" or the "priest", was proud and overbearing, and had managed to make that quite clear during a political discussion "about a month before" his death. He had gone as far as to promote himself intellectually above "God".

As the speaker concludes his reflection, he reinforces the "peoples" dedication to religion and the "priest" on the "island". The persona lets us know that the effect of the lawyer's "arrogant" comments momentarily froze his audience and gave them an eerie feeling. The moment passed but 'things' were not the same. So, now it is strongly felt that this accident has been the act of "God" against this lawyer.

There is, of course, a strong atmosphere of superstition sustained throughout the narrative and this is in tandem with supernatural beliefs—not just that there is a superior spiritual force or power to be feared, but when disrespected or irrevered, this can lead to disastrous results. Also, the site of the accident evokes the uncanny, as on a "wide, straight road, bright bright / middle day, [and] not another car in sight" the dead man's "brains" is found some distance "just like / somebody take it up careful careful / and put it by itself" from the rest of his body. Thus, the persona describes the situation as "a damn funny thing". The sense of shock is strongly evoked by comparing the knowledge and impact of the shock to that of "the whole island catch[ing] sunstroke".

The diction of "The Accident" is emphatic, complementing the heightened sense of disbelief and wonder in the persona's voice. The image of the lawyer is that of an "island" resident who has achieved accomplishments enough to set him apart from the ordinary folk, being an "Island Scholar" who has returned as a lawyer, but also lacking in humility. The first verse sets the tone with "damn" and stresses are in the use of "bright bright" and "careful careful", for example. The mixture of the vernacular with the standard by the speaker suggests that the speaker is one who is readily able to identify with the simple folk and is able to move back and forth on a continuum. The first two verses have frequent use of exclamation marks which effectively raise the tone, whether it be that of the persona, or the lawyer's sharp response. However, the tone of the last verse is lowered in contrast as the mood of the speaker changes to conclude the matter with folk wisdom and insight, again reinforcing the incomprehensibility of the "accident".

Another poem that evokes stark death is the two-part ironic "Amadou's Mother" (29). The first part of "Amadou's Mother" is "Mother Liberty Speaks" and the second part is "Kandiatou Diallo Speaks" (30). Two sides are told of the same story.

In the first part of the story "Mother Liberty" invites destitute persons to come to her and be killed by the "gun" in "Brooklyn" and "Bronx" in the middle of the night by "Angels of the Law", in her "holy" name. She then makes reference to one of her victims—"a nigger"—who was killed in "fair[ness]" as this was what was necessary in order to save the "town" from "fear". The voice continues in a harsh note to describe the reactions of the victims during the killing—"pissing their pants". This male "nigger" died among them and he had come in response to "Mother Liberty['s]" beckoning, and for reasons similar to others before him who had followed the "dream".

The second part of the story (30) is set in a "courtroom". The speaker says that from the beginning of the trial it was apparent that the subject of the trial was absent and that this realization was not due to the fact that the subject was "dead" and so could not tell "his story"; it was because of the testimony being given by the "cops". The four "neatly dressed" cops were explaining about their emotional distress and pleas to the victim before his death. The persona comments that they "have made a desert of my heart" so that it will only be possible to forgive when the "truth" is told. The persona ends the account by stating the relation to the dead boy—he was the persona's son.

In the first account, the caption "Mother Liberty Speaks" (29) alludes to the Statue of Liberty, and this knowledge is grounded by the reference to "Brooklyn and the Bronx" that are New York cities in North America. However, the idea of "Liberty" is ironically overturned as the opening dramatically presents the stark reality of ruthlessness that can be experienced in the named cities. Not only are the "hungry" and the "poor" who come to the vicinities of the statue in search of "Liberty" killed, but the speaker evokes the idea of mindless persecution as the killing is done "in their doorways" by "Angels of the Law". The representation of "[l]iberty", then, is seen as false, and the "Angels of the Law" is a sarcastic and interrogatory metaphor of the perversion of justice.

There is a sense of double vision in the personification of "Mother Liberty". The words spoken are words 'given' to "Mother Liberty" and the speaker is deconstructing the original (first) symbolism and reconstructing a new narrative with the vision and diction of one who sees American "[l]iberty" as exclusive of the non-white race. The boy killed "was only a nigger"—where "only" depicts insignificance, and "nigger" is the derogatory for negro or African. The excess of violence is depicted by "forty-one bullets", and the kneeling as mock reverence. Ruthless extermination is the 'freedom' that is gained by the negro who seeks the "[l]iberty" of "Brooklyn" and "Bronx", and the speaker subverts the idea of ethnic tolerance.

The situation in part two of the story is set in a "courtroom". The "cops" are on trial for the death of "Amadou" whose harsh killing is told in part one of the story. Amadou is the son of "Kandiatou Diallo", the speaker. Although the graphic details of the murder are not rehashed in this part of the story, the link is clear in the allusion to "Miss America's sons" who "taint[ed] their hands / with his blood". The metaphoric "made a desert of my heart" underscores the sense of desolation and depredation infused into the speaker by the testimony of the "neatly dressed cops in the dock". Seeing that the persona does not recognize any "truth" in the testimony, the conclusion must be drawn that the "cops" are seen to be speaking lies. The sense of injustice in the killing is indicated when the speaker says: "He was only a boy going home".

On another view of death, "Obituary Page" (35) leaves little for the imagination to ponder. This poem is a dramatic monologue in which the speaker, who identifies herself at the very end as "Mavis", expresses her concerns about the manner in which a person's death is communicated. She is disgruntled that instead of just hearing the word "die", what she is hearing are ideas and phrases used as substitutes. She gives examples of some of these words and phrases. Her complaint takes a humorous twist of the idea of "passed"—questioning the reason that the person had not "stop[ped]". She concludes that whenever her time comes and she is dead, others should be told in a straightforward manner: "Mavis dead".

This poem really gives a lesson in the use of euphemism. "Obituary Page" could be further interpreted as the very page on which the poem is printed, not just that of a newspaper's announcement of death. Having established that the topic is death, the speaker reveals varying connotated language that function to mitigate the harsh reality of death. The humour evoked by the dramatic telling functions also as a mask for the discomfiting effect. Notwithstanding, the persona tells us that the truth is unavoidable in the final pronouncement of "Mavis Dead".

CRITICAL THINKING

13. How would you know if a place or person mentioned in a poem has significance, or is real?

    a. Look at the poem "When the Doomed are Most Eloquent in their Sinking" (38). How does the name "(*Malcolm Lowry*)"assist you in your analysis?

    b. What difference would it have made if the person were not named?

14. What is the mood of "Holy Fever" (41)? How does the word "God" assist you in your analysis?

DESIRE, YEARNING, AND REGRET

One may ask, "What exactly is desire?" From a literary critic's standpoint, Baugh had something to say about desire in "Literary Theory And The Caribbean: Theory, Belief And Desire, or Designing Theory".[91] This was an address in which a lot of retrospection was done in looking back at what was not, and what could have been—which concisely and succinctly identifies desire and regret. Where desire is concerned (in his address), the term captures what Baugh wants to see happen—a wish for a particular kind of reality or manifestation which could "influence"(11) [92] the world. Even though Baugh was arguing for a particular Caribbean theory, we can expect no less than to see the essence of this idea in his work. For, it is Baugh who reminds us that "Writing . . . is a construction of identity . . ."[93] (2004). When desire is unfulfilled, it can develop in intensity and evolve into a state of yearning. This section will explore the idea of longing for a reality that could change things, circumstances, or people, and the sadness that often accompanies retrospection.

One poem evoking wistfulness and aspects of desire is "Black Sand" (16). From the very first line, the poem starts a long series of "if[s]" like a restless pedant pursued by a nagging difficulty. The speaker takes a deep and imaginative look at elements of nature and human relations, measuring the insight each aspect reveals against the limitation of "the poem".

The most outstanding figurative device used is the simile. But, with every simile that is used, the intensity in the mood increases. This poem's parallel can be appreciated in "What's Poetry For" (24) as it seems to be addressing the difficulty that many persons experience in the search for meaning and interpretation in poetry, thus leaving them oftentimes baffled. The persona evokes a Romantic imagination in describing the phenomenal capacity and beauty of "black sand", infusing wonder and reverence. This deep study of "black sand" depicts the deepening of the desire that a form of art, such as a poem, should be able to yield to the imagination, an understanding and interpretation of itself as one becomes "absorb[ed]" in its contents and exercises "patien[ce]". Then, one could delight in poetry, as a "woman" delights in "wavelets [that]

91. Plenary Address, 2nd Caribbean Culture Conference UWI, Cave Hill "(Re)Thinking Caribbean Culture," June 4-8, 2001.
92. JWIL (2001)
93. 23rd ACWIL

splash over her feet" and be able to study it "without fear". Even as our contact with nature impacts positively on us, so should our contact with poetry be, time and time again. There is a nuance of regret that is strengthened with the repetitive "if", and the speaker ends, but the voice is resonant with an unlikely possibility.

The next poem, "Out of Stock" (52), is a dramatic monologue. In it the indignant speaker is addressing a woman with an endearing title—"Chile". The persona is questioning her friend whether the situation she is unhappy about has ever been her friend's experience. For, whenever she goes shopping as, for example, in the previous week when she went shopping for "bathroom tiles", as soon as she chose and ordered the "tile" on display she was told that it was "out of stock". She wants her friend to tell her why persons continue to display goods that are unavailable. She thinks that the practice should be outlawed and if she had the "power" she would do it. The speaker continues in saying that the occurrence repeats itself in her experiences with men, for no sooner does she "see a good one" who is perfect for her than she is told that he is 'out of stock'.

The allegorical anecdote given by the speaker suggests that she is a person who is haunted by unfulfilled desires and that the real source of her troubles is that of the unavailability of eligible males. Humour masks the sense of missed opportunities and regret for having heard "out of stock".

Next, there is a mocking of the 'prim and proper' in "Miss Lady is Weeping" (49). The speaker tells us that "Miss Lady . . ." is sitting down in "her favourite chair" and the tears are flowing without making any noise, so that you would not know unless you were to look directly "into her face". The reason for the tears is "a knot of pain" in her lower abdomen. The woman has decided that she will remain in that position until late into the night for it is around that time that "He" will appear and give her the comfort she needs. She will take him in her arms, and it is then that her crying will stop.

This poem leaves very little to challenge the imagination. The "weeping" evokes the depth of "Miss Lady[s] . . ." distress, and though she is sitting down appearing 'prim', she cannot escape the raw cut of her sexuality. "[M]idnight" encourages the thought of a clandestine relationship between "He" and her, and whether it is a necessity that she has to let him in. On all accounts, the situation is questionable.

Also striking a sexual note is "Home Truths" (54). In this poem the woman is remembering how she took instructions from her mother as a "girl" on how to "make [her] bed" in order to keep her "husband". Now as she "straighten[s] the spread" while her "lover" prepares himself to leave, she mentally addresses her mother, thinking about how she has not been able to find a "husband".

On one level, "Home Truths" can be seen as a matter of fact statement—a convention of childrearing. But, the other truth is that even though one may be well prepared through training, this does not guarantee a husband, or even a faithful one who "wouldn't / leave". Thus, the title is as ambiguous as it is ironic.

A similar poem to "Home Truths" is "True Love" (50), also a dramatic monologue. The speaker is addressing someone and acknowledging the "lament" of the second person concerning the brevity of the visits. The speaker visits, makes love, and then leaves. But, the second person's desire is to have the lover spend the night so that they can wake up together on the morning after.

It is debatable whether the speaker is a man or woman. An interpretation of the speaker's sex likely depends on the cultural norm of the reader. Seeing, however, that it is the female who usually "command[s]" love making with "passion / and . . . tenderness", it is reasonable to interpret the speaker as a man, or masculine. The desire of the listener is for a sustainable partnership. However, it appears that the speaker is using what is a reality of life and natural for relationships—"break wind, and belch, and snore"—as a flimsy excuse to avoid the commitment and companionship the second person desires.

When the three foregoing poems are analysed in this order, a kind of sequel emerges. We can see a woman—"Miss Lady . . ."—sitting and waiting in tears for a late night visit by her lover. Then, after the lovemaking is done, in "Home Truths", the woman is thoughtfully re-making the bed as the man prepares to leave. But, a "lament" emerges in "True Love" as the woman continues to grapple with the absence of true partnership.

Critical Thinking

15. a. In what way is "Black Sand" (16) similar to "Memories Like Comfort Stones" (45)?

    b. What figure of speech is outstanding in "Memories . . ."?

16. Study "River Song" (48) carefully. What nuances in the poem suggest desire? What suggests that the desire had been fulfilled?

PART FOUR

FURTHER STUDIES IN:

Further Studies in

CRITICAL READING, THINKING AND WRITING

17. More on Anderson's theory of renaming.

Also, in his discussion on 'old' and 'new', Anderson outlines the conditions required for this kind of parallelism or coexistence (of cities) to be realized and portray political significance. It was necessary that "the distance between the parallel groups be large, and that the newer of them be substantial in size and permanently settled, as well as, firmly subordinated to the older" (188). The parallel with the poems under study is that the subjects are drawn from the larger, older experience and presented in their condensed poetic form from which a variety of perceptions can be drawn.

However, this concept of memory (by Anderson) does not have a parallel in all of Baugh's poetry. For instance, the muse enables the evocation and re-creation of the mechanism of enslavement in "Sometimes in the Middle of the Story" in memory of the drowned Africans who lost their lives in the Atlantic sea. This poem, though a combination of myth and fact, is a poignant artistic materialization of remembrance as muse. This is a poem which also draws on intellectual experience—being shaped into form from the recorded or remembered history of the burden of African-Caribbean people in the New World. This aspect of the manifestation of the 'pioneering' spirit of the colonizer goes beyond Anderson's theoretical boundary. As Anderson notes:

> [t]he brutal mechanisms of slavery ensured not merely [the] political-cultural fragmentation, [of the African immigrant population] but also very rapidly removed the possibility of imagining black communities in Venezuela and West Africa moving in parallel trajectory. (189)

It is a statement which reinforces the perception that where immigration and enslavement via the Atlantic ocean are concerned, this parallelism or synchronic renaming has had a greater agenda—that of imperialism or colonialism. In this context, the significant link being made with Anderson's theory is the transfer of African experience into art form, re-naming, as well as, instituting these artistic representations as artefacts in poetic form. So, the exclusion in Anderson's theory of renaming, caused by history and colonialism's 'othering' of the black race, is ingeniously filled by Baugh.

18. More on the Romantic Imagination

The cadre of poets classified as the Romantics were likely influenced by contemporary philosophical teachings which stressed the worth of the individual and the function of the imagination. These poets are best known as William Blake, Samuel Taylor Coleridge, John Keats, William Wordsworth, Percy Bysshe Shelley and George Byron. C. M. Bowra (1973) explains that Romantics believe that "physical things must be embraced by some sustaining power [and] their senses set their visionary powers into action" (12).

Kristi Pritchett[94] also explains that this 'ideological turn' in literary attitude and craft was a reaction to the effects of the Industrial Revolution—hence, a resistance to change and a yearning for the past which affected all the arts. Samuel Taylor Coleridge and William Wordsworth, for example, placed emphasis on simple language and commonplace subjects, emotion, self-revelation, and celebrated the bond between nature and the human mind. It was during this era that the traditional sonnets lost their appeal and variations emerged. In particular, Wordsworth was influential in 'freeing' the sonnet from the subject of love only.

As you re-read Baugh's poetry, examine the extent to which Baugh's work evokes Romanticism.

94. Of Columbus State University

SAMPLE QUESTIONS: CRITICAL READING, THINKING, WRITING

19. **Instruction: Write a critical response for as many as possible, of the challenges given below. Ask a peer, or an instructor to evaluate your answers.**

a. "Poetic autobiography, complex and subjective though it may be, has a certain value." With reference to at least three poems in *Black Sand,* analyse the subject and structure of each that validate them as more than just autobiography.

b. With reference to at least three poems in *Black Sand,* discuss the extent to which you agree with the necessity to re-create collective history.

c. "Understanding remembrance as muse is integral for an overall appreciation of Baugh's poetry." Discuss the function of memory as a tool for sustainable living and development. In your answer make close reference to at least three poems in *Black Sand.*

d. "Baugh is not 'chained' to poetic conventions." With close reference to the overall structure of at least three poems in *Black Sand*, discuss the extent to which you agree with the foregoing statement.

e. "Nation is not static, but is transportable." Write a close reading response to the foregoing view, referring to at least three poems in *Black Sand.*

f. Read the poem "Black Sand" and then answer the questions below.

  (i) What particular diction does the poet use as a technique to suggest a challenge or limitation of "the poem"?

  (ii) Name the technique employed in (i). Explain its effectiveness on the overall mood of the poem.

  (iii) What figure of speech is used repeatedly by the speaker in expressing an overall ambition for "the poem"?

  (iv) What effect does the use of imagery have on the imagination? Explain in detail.

  (v) The speaker juxtaposes poetry against nature. What conclusions might be drawn from this contrast?

GLOSSARY

Glossary

Charles-atlas shoulders: An allusion to the strength of "Yard Boy" by evoking the memory of **Charles Atlas**, born **Angelo Siciliano** (October 30, 1892– December 23, 1972) who successfully changed himself from a skinny young man into a renowned bodybuilder. The original Atlas is a Greek mythical character (a titan) which was punished with the task of upholding "the canopy of heaven".

Blackheart Man: A man (of folk memory) who would drive through communities and snatch children who strayed from home, stayed out late, or were guilty of other mischief.

Blake: William Blake, Romantic poet.

Bosun: Also, boatswain. A ship's officer who is in charge of equipment and crew.

Catherine's Peak: A peak in the Blue Mountains range.

Diaspora culture: Life customs of Africans, or ethnographic practices re-enacted in their new setting.

Dramatic monologue: A poem in which one speaker speaks to an audience, whether imagined or real but it is one sided.

East Harbour: Kingston harbour to the east.

Elegy: A poem lamenting the death of someone, originally written in elegiac meter—alternating hexameter and pentameter lines.

Epiphany: A moment of spiritual awakening.

Errol Flynn: Australian movie star who rose to fame around the mid twentieth century as a swashbuckler.

Ethos: Attitudes of a culture or community, accepted norms.

Idiom of the Jamaican folk: Peculiar mannerism and speech related to Jamaican culture.

Interior monologue: An aspect of stream of consciousness in which the writer presents the preoccupations of the character's mind as they unfold, without interruption.

Jamaica: Caribbean island, place of Edward Baugh's birth. According to historian Ansell Hart, the name is formed by the Indians who came to the island from South America millennia ago—"chabauan" means water, "makia" means wood, first forming "chabmakia". The Spaniards' tongue evolved it into "chamakia", spelled "xaymaca". Columbus' compatriot, wanted to rename the island to honour patron Saint James of Spain, but his fellowman, Acosta, disputed St Jago and called the island Jamaycque. It was eventually adjusted to Jamaica by another countryman, Benzo.

Jamaican folklife: The customs or conventions of 'ordinary' Jamaicans, especially those with simple living practices and a preferred closeness to nature.

Junction Road: A winding road in the hilly areas of north St Andrew, leading to St Mary.

Juxtaposition: Contrasting images against each other in order to emphasize an understanding.

Kingston: Capital city of Jamaica.

Kintyre: A district in St Andrew, Jamaica.

Lignum Vitae: A tree which blooms Jamaica's national flower.

Norwich: A small town in Portland, Jamaica.

Odes: Lyric poems generally written in elevated, elaborate style. In this case "Yard Boy" is a praise poem and has nuances of Pindar's odes. However, its tone is just about all in the similarity.

Oral culture: Narratives passed down through generations by word of mouth.

Orality: The particular nature of written words that need to be sounded out, voiced, otherwise performed for greater understanding of the context in which they are being used.

Port Royal: Originally named Caguaya by the Spaniards, Port Royal is the first most important town of the Spanish era, then city after the English took over; the town became a haven for buccaneers, famous for its wealth, but was first sunken by a massive earthquake in 1692.

Portland: Eastern parish in Jamaica noted for banana agriculture and export hub.

Postcolonial evocations: References to European influence and control of Jamaica, as well as, other islands in the Caribbean Sea, during and after colonization.

Rio Grande: A river that meanders along the base of the John Crow Mountains to sea at Port Antonio, capital of the parish of Portland.

Romanticized: Given an image of perfection, or told in a way as to suggest the ideal.

Sonnet: A lyric poem of one stanza of fourteen lines written in iambic pentameter with a strict rhyme scheme. The major types are Italian or Petrarchan, and English or Shakespearean, but there is also a variant called Spenserian.

Trans-Atlantic Slave Trade: The infamous transfer of enslaved Africans across the Atlantic.

Wag Water: A river running through northern St. Andrew and St. Mary—parishes in Jamaica.

Warner-Woman: A real preacher woman, wrapped in long flourishing garments, and wearing a head wrap in which items such as pencils and feathers are stuck.

***Zacca*:** The name of a ship.

WORKS CITED

Abrams, M. H. *A Glossary of Literary Terms.* 6th ed. Forth Worth: Harcourt Brace College Publishers, 1993. 123, 283. Print.

Achebe, Chinua. *Things Fall Apart.* London: Heinemann, 1985. Print.

Anderson, Benedict. "Memory and Forgetting." *Imagined Communities.* Revised edition. London: Verso, 2006. 187-206. Print.

Ashcroft, Bill, Gareth Griffiths and Helen Tiffin. *The Empire Writes Back.* 2nd ed. London: Routledge, 2003. Print.

Bakhtin, Mikhail M. *The Dialogic Imagination.* Ed. Michael Holquist. Trans. Caryl Emerson and Michael Holquist. Austin: University of Texas Press, 2002. Print.

Baugh, Edward. "Confessions of a Critic." *Journal of West Indian Literature,* 15.1-2 (November 2006) 15-28. Print.

---. Review of *Another Life* by Derek Walcott. *Caribbean Quarterly* 21.3 *(Sept. 1975)*: 58-59. Print.

---. *Derek Walcott: Memory as Vision: Another Life*. London: Longman, *1978. Print.*

---. *It Was the Singing.* Toronto: Sandberry Press, 2000. Print.

---. "Literary Theory And The Caribbean: Theory, Belief And Desire, or Designing Theory." *Journal of West Indian Literature,* 15.1-2 (November 2006) 3-14. Print.

Benítez-Rojo, Antonio. *The Repeating Island: The Caribbean and the Postmodern Perspective.* 2nd ed. Trans. James E. Maraniss. Durham and London: Duke University Press, 2001. Print.

Bennett, Andrew and Nicholas Royle. *Introduction to Literature, Criticism and Theory*. 2nd ed. London: Prentice Hall Europe, 1999. Print.

Bowra, C. M. *The Romantic Imagination*. London: Oxford University Press, 1973. Print.

Brathwaite, Kemau. *The Arrivants*. Oxford: Oxford Univ. Press, 1998. Print.

Breiner, Laurence A. *An Introduction to West Indian Poetry*. Cambridge: Cambridge University Press, 1998. Print.

Edwards, Nadi. "Edward Baugh: The Critic as Mediator." *Journal of West Indian Literature*, 15.1-2 (November 2006) 33-54. Print.

Fanon, Frantz. *The Wretched of the Earth*. London: Penguin Books Ltd., 2001. Print.

Foucault, Michel. "The Archaeology of Knowledge" (1969). *Literary Theory: An Anthology*. Ed. Julie Rivkin,and Michael Ryan. Malden: Blackwell Publishing, 2003. 421-428. Print.

Grinam-Nicholson, Yvonne. "Professor Edward Baugh: Living the Years." *Outlook Sunday Magazine*. Kingston: The Gleaner Company Ltd., 2001. 9 -12. Print.

Hart, Ansell. "Monthly Comments. Jamaica." Vol. 5. No. 1. (August 1962-July 1964). March 2001. Web. March 23, 2007.

IMDb.com, Inc. "Biography for Errol Flynn." Web. 23 Sept. 2013.

Ismond, Patricia. "Another Life: Autobiography as Alternative History." *Journal of West Indian Literature* 4.1 (January 1990): 41-49. Print.

King, Bruce, ed. *West Indian Literature*. London: The Macmillan Press, Ltd., 1979. Print.

Mda, Zakes. *Ways of Dying*. New York: Farrar, Straus and Giroux, 1991. 30. Print.

Narloch, Tony. "Greek mythology: Atlas." Helium.com. 14 June 2009. Web. 23 Sept. 2013.

Pritchett, Kristi. "The Romantic Period." Columbus State University. Web. 24 Sept. 2013.

Renan, Ernest. "What is a nation? (1882)." Trans. and annot. Martin Thom. *Nation and Narration*. Ed. Homi K. Bhabha. London: Routledge, 2007. 8-22. Print.

Rohlehr, Gordon. "The Folk in Caribbean Literature." *Critics on Caribbean Literature*. Ed. Edward Baugh. London: George Allen and Unwin Ltd., 1978. 27-30. Print.

---. "The Problem of the Problem of Form: The Idea of an Aesthetic Continuum and Aesthetic Code-switching in West Indian Literature." *The Shape That Hurt and other essays*. Port of Spain: Longman Trinidad Limited, 1992. 1-65. Print.

Walcott, Derek. "The Muse of History." *Critics on Caribbean Literature*. Ed. Edward Baugh. London: George Allen & Unwin (Publishers) Ltd., 1978. 38-43. Print.

Walcott, Derek. "Derek Walcott on West Indian Literature and Theatre." Interview with Edward Baugh. *Jamaica Journal* 21.2 (1988): 50-52. Print.

Helpful links for research on Edward Baugh

http://www.poetryarchive.org/poetryarchive/singlePoet.do?poetId=14978

This link has readings by Baugh himself
http://www.spaceswords.com/?page_id=110

This link has an interesting interview with Prof. Baugh and other treats.
http://www.caribbean-beat.com/issue-81/edward-baugh-%E2%80%9Chey-you-might-be-poet%E2%80%9D

An article.
http://streaming.miami.edu:8080/ramgen/artscience/cariblitstudies/1995/1995_P05_02_poemset1.rm

Edward Baugh reads poetry about parents and childhood (1995)

www.ingramcontent.com/pod-product-compliance
Lightning Source LLC
Chambersburg PA
CBHW032027040426
42448CB00006B/751